INSIDE OUT

KENNETH A. RICHARDS

One of my fondest memories of being a little boy was when my mother would come into my room in the morning and sit on the side of my bed. She would sit there as she would look in the chest of drawers to pick out the clothes that she would dress me in that day. I especially liked the cold mornings. I remember that when she would sit on the side of my bed her weight would make the mattress go down on that side. This would make my skinny little four year old body move closer to her. Mom would be wearing her thick purple housecoat with the belt left untied. Why she never tied the belt on her housecoat I do not know. But, what I do know is that when I would wrap my skinny little body around her warm hips it felt absolutely wonderful! Cold mornings were the best!

I was an only child at that time. Life was so simple and sweet for me then. Mama would get me up in the morning. She and I would spend the day together and after the mailman would come I knew that it would not be long before daddy's car would pull into the driveway. Daddy would come through the front door and pick me up with his strong arm and rub the gritty stubble of his chin into my belly. He would kiss mama and then go take his bath. And as my mother would finish up with making supper I would set the table with folded napkins and silverware. Then when everything was set mama would say,"Go get your dad". I would run to the bedroom and shout,"Daddy its ready"! We would sit down together at the dinner table and when we said the grace we did it with a song, "God is great and God is good, and we thank him for our food. By his hands we all are fed; give us Lord our daily bread. AMEN". Yep! Life was sweet and simple and good.

Before he became my dad one day he was walking home after a long day of working in the field. And as he walked down the rocky red clay road of the Jamaican countryside he saw a large group of people running towards him. He could not tell what they were saying but he did recognize them as the people of his village. The entire village was running to meet him! It was the teenage boys and young men that got to him first. They surrounded him grabbing his arms and patting him on the back as they all jumped around him with great enthusiasm! They lifted him to their shoulders and began to run carrying him back to the others of his village. And then he could hear them clearly. Many people with one clear voice saying over and over, "Uncle Randall, you going U.S." Surely he must be dreaming! But, who had told them that? Why him? He was 26 years of age and had never been more than 10 miles from the little country house he was born in! He did not even have shoes how could he be going to America?

This was 1951 and things were very different than they

are today. Back then character, honor, and respect were not just words. They meant something! My dad told me that unbeknownst to him the U.S. Sugar Corporation had sent representatives to Jamaica to find workers for sugar plantations in south Florida. These representatives would go to each Parrish and find the most respected person in the area. They gave that person a card to be filled out and on that card they wanted the name of the one young man that the respected person would trust.

Father told me that two weeks before he was to depart for America he was summoned by a great old lady in his Parrish. She being from a good family that was well respected. She told him that she remembered when he was born. But, not only that! She also remembered when his parents were born! She said to him in her rich Jamaican patios, "Me know you! You have a certain character! Clean & Nice"! She told him that it was this certain character that he had which made her put his name on the card. I would come to find out just what that really meant later on in my own life. Somehow just a bit of his strong character was passed on to me. And in my darkest hour when I thought that all was lost it was daddy's teachings that saved my life.

A sable colored young woman from the poorest part of Jim Crow Virginia boarded a train one Sunday afternoon. She was alone. All that she owned was in one little travel bag. She had a $5.00 bill safety-pinned on the inside of her brassiere. She didn't have much but she had all that she needed! She had faith in God and a determination to be more than what she was. Both of these would be put to the test.

After college this young lady who would one day be my mother was sent to Kentucky for her first teaching assignment. Mother told me that, "Both the white folks and the Black folks didn't know what to make of me"! Mother was always good with words. I can just imagine a skinny little coal black woman all of 116 lbs speaking in a manner that sounded like she knew what she was talking about. And in a tone that sounded like she believed what she was saying!

She did her best while on her Kentucky assignment but all those years she dreamed of a warmer climate where the people felt more like the folks back at home. She dreamed of a husband, a house of her own, and a little boy like me.

Then one day see received a telegram that said, "Transferring you to south Florida...your replacement arrives next Monday...be ready to travel next Tuesday...Ticket at train station. She thought it had to be a dream! She had wanted this for so long! And now her dream was about to be fulfilled! Favor had smiled down on her and she was grateful.

If the writer of that telegram had only known they could have also told her that she was being sent ahead to establish a territory, to put down some roots, to make ready! For he who knows all was soon to transfer to her the husband she dreamed of.

And in a little while they would make me. And we would be the happy three living in the little house that she wanted so much.

When I was a little boy I had the best of everything! What's so funny about it now is that I had no idea during those young years that I was a little rich kid with all kinds of wealth! Firstly, I had both of my parents and we lived together in a cozy little house. I had a dad who was hard working and paid our bills. I had a mom who cooked all sorts of health dishes from scratch. From the age of three I went to work with my father and he taught me the gift of working hard. I remember one day when I was about five years old and dad and I were traveling from one job to another. Out of nowhere dad says to me in a low and very serious Jamaican voice, "Kennet, work is a blessing you know"! So, I had a live-in work coach who not only taught me how to do different task but also would threaten to give me a whipping if the task was not done to his liking. Rich indeed! My mother loved public speaking. She was the teacher of grades 1 – 6 at our Church School and she believed that any and every child could learn. So guess who did a whole lot of public speaking as a little boy? Me! Whenever someone had a program at church or at school and they needed a child to speak I was always volunteered. Mom believed in preparation. All week long before I was to perform, she and I would practice together. There was always a tree branch called a switch nearby during these practice sessions. But my riches don't stop there! When I was five years old I had my first flight on an air plane and my first travel abroad! Dad and I went to visit Jamaica and I met my father's family and mine for the first time! WOW, as I am writing this I just had an incredible flashback! The morning of this trip to Jamaica my mother, father, and I got into a taxi-cab which took us to the Trailways Bus Station. Dad and I were seated on the bus and we were looking out at mother as she looked back at us. Suddenly, my father got up out of his seat and said something to the bus driver. He then got off of the bus and walked up to my mother. And then, right outside the window where I was sitting my parents leapt into each other's arms and my father kissed her. Not the kind of light peak on the lips that I had witnessed many times before. His lips seemed to be trying to pull her into himself! It was like the way he tried to get the last drop of juice out of an orange when he ate one! And she my sweet little mother was yielding herself to this madman that father had become! I was in shock! What had I just witnessed?

But, I digress. What I was telling you is that as a kid I had so much! I had real wealth! No, not the kind you keep in a bank. I had that wealth that comes from God and nature. The wealth of a good man and a good woman coming together and giving all that they had to the little new life that they had made together.

One of the things that really bothered mother was when my hair started to get too long for her liking. She would say, "Boy, you startin' to look wooly headed. Take this $2.00 and go get your hair cut"! At that time mom was teaching at our church's school. Our church and the school were on Parramore Street which was that street where almost anything and everything could and usually did happen. On one side of our church was a restaurant and on the other side was the barber shop. I take the $2.00 from mother's hand and the last thing that she tells me is, "Tell him to take it down real low. These haircuts have got to last awhile"! I get to the barber shop and I am the only person there. The barber was a smooth looking slim older man. This cat was always so neat and clean. I get in the chair and tell him what mama had said. As he is cutting my hair a pretty young lady comes in the front door and smiles at the barber. She asked him if she can have a private word with him and being the kind gentleman that he is he tells her yes. He spins the chair around so that I am facing that long mirror across the back of the shop and together they go through the gold curtain that leads to the back room.

I had no idea what a private word was but I could not hear any talking. As I sat there I realized that I had never really seen the shop from this angle. It was really beautiful! There were all these tall glass bottles with gold, and green, and red colored hair stuff! There were cans of talc with a well dressed Englishmen on the cover! All of the big mirrors were framed in florescent lights! And at both ends of the long counter there were red, white, and blue barber poles encased in glass! I sat there marveling at how cool everything looked! And then I looked down.

There was a drawer that had been left open and as I looked down into it I saw what looked like pictures of women without any clothes on! My eyes got bigger than they already were and my heart started to beat faster! I got down out of the chair and I was just tall enough to see into the drawer. There must have been a hundred or more little black and white photographs there. I was in little boy heaven! I quickly grabbed one of the pictures and put it in my pocket. Almost the second that I got back into the chair the young lady and the barber came back into the shop!

I was so in love with that picture. This flat thin little piece of four square inches became my most prized possession. I thought about it all the time. Just knowing that it was hidden in my mother's car gave me great joy. My mother would be on the telephone with one of her girlfriends gossiping and I would be out in her car having mindsex with the little naked Goddess in the picture. I was obsessed with her image! That's what addicts do! We are obsessed beings! And that's what I had become. That's what I would be. I just didn't even know what that was yet.

One of the highlights of my young life was Camp meeting. We were church people and that's what we did. For two weeks every year mother and I would go to Hawthorne, Florida and camp-out in the name of the Lord! Dad would be there for both weekends. He went home to work through the week. I enjoyed all of the experience so very much! That whole week before the three of us would be preparing to go off on our adventure! And then the day would arrive and I would help dad pack the car. When all was ready we would bow our heads and say a prayer and be on our way! Mother and father would be in the front seat talking about grown folks stuff. And I was in the back seat with wide-eyed wonder taking in all the sights along the way.

Camp meeting was singing songs of Jesus, it was arts and crafts, it was sampling different foods at the book store, hiking, swimming, and of course it was about camping. But, it was so much more than that! It was an opportunity to get away from man made things and get back to nature. No running water. Cooking over a fire made from wood chips that we would gather. Living in tents and sleeping on little fold-out cots. And using a whole lot of a mosquito spray called "6-12".

It was at one camp meeting that I realized that I wanted a wife. I wanted someone to be by my side so that we could talk about grown folks stuff when we went on trips together. I think I was six years old at the time. I saw a girl one day while we were coloring pictures of Jesus and the angels. She was a little angel herself. Her hair was done in three thick twists. She always wore a pinafore dress with a white blouse. She wore sandals and pretty turned down socks. She was kinda bossy but I didn't care. I wondered if she would be my wife. After all I had my own room with bunk beds. And I had a little desk that would be perfect for her to color pictures on.

I was very nerdy around the time of my 13th birthday. The adolescent years were tough and very unkind to me. I was a skinny and very shy early teenager. My mother still bought my clothes for me then and they were always two sizes too big. Mother told me that what was important was that my body was covered not how I looked. "Besides, you'll grow into them", she would tell me. I thought that she really didn't care about me. I know now that she didn't have the money to buy me nice things.

My parents were firm literal believers of the Holy Bible and they thought that Jesus was coming not only very soon but at any minute. Because of this they kept me close to home. My early years were a cycle of school, chores, working with dad, church, and working with dad again. I was not allowed to play with but a very few neighborhood kids and my view of life and the world around me was very limited.

The street that I grow up on had a quiet end and a loud active end. I lived on the quiet end. On the other end of my street there were many boys about my same age.

These boys would be playing in the street all the time and it looked like they were having so much fun! I could not go down there to the other end so I would stand just past the sidewalk on the grass in front of my house and watch them. I wanted to go down there and run and jump and shout gleefully just as the other young boys were doing but mother always said no.

Then one day I asked mom if I could go down the street and she said yes! But, there were conditions to this answer of yes. All my chores had to be done and I had to take a bath, comb and brush my hair, and put on some decent clothes. I was so excited about my adventure of going down the street to play with the other young boys that I was beside myself! I rushed through my chores took a bath and got dressed. I came into the living room for mom to inspect me and she told me that I had missed a belt loop. She then told me not to scuff-up my shoes and to keep my shirt tail tucked in.

I walked what must have been 75 yards to the other end of my street where the boys my age were playing and just stood there and watched with wide-eyed wonder as they played two-hand touch football! They ran and jumped, and shouted at each other and I was amazed! They were playing and I was right there up close watching them! Not on my end of the street but rather right down there on the other end where there was fun!

As I watched the dozen or so boys playing this two-hand touch one of them asked me if I lived down the street and I said, "Yes"! They all stopped sudden and began to look at each other. After a little while they all began saying YES to each other and snickering. Then another kid asked me if I was on my way to church? It was then that I noticed that none of them had on any shirts. They weren't wearing any shoes either! And there I stood in my long sleeve dress shirt, my khaki slacks, and my wingtip shoes saying YES. Needless to say I did not fit in with these soon to be new friends of mine.

8

Fitting in was not something that was important to my parents. Both of my parents were strong minded, strong willed folks who marched to the beat of their own individual drummers. My father was a foreigner to this country and he was who he was and that was that. Mother had a college degree in a time when this was a rare thing. It made her vision different from most of the others around us. My father would take a break in the middle of his first job to come home in the morning to have worship with us before we left for school. The whole family would be together in the living room singing songs about Jesus and his love. The lifestyle we lived made for continuous questions by my peers. They would ask me, "Why do y'all be sanging church songs in the morning and it ain't even Sunday", and "What is that funny food that you be eating", they would say, "Why your daddy talk so funny" or, "Do you have to ask your mother for permission every time you go somewhere"? The questions about me being and living a different way were never ending. One boy asked a question of my one day that kind of said it best. He simply asked me, "Who you suppose to be"? I was dumbfounded! I didn't really understand the question but I knew that he was saying, "You're not one of us". I felt so bad inside. I so wanted to fit in.

So let's see now. I'm 13 years of age. I am tall for my age but very skinny. I am beyond shy and insecure. I wear bifocal glasses and none of my clothes fit. I go to church on the Sabbath which is on Saturday. Slang is forbidden in my household so I don't know any of the cool things to say even if I had the courage to say them. I was beginning to like girls but no girl would dare to talk to me. I had no big brother or big sister to pave the way for me and give me status or clout. And, I brought my lunch to school from home when everyone else got their food in the school cafeteria. I was alone and lonely. Why can't I just be like everyone else?

I was not who I wanted to be. Neither did I have the things that I wished for. But, I did have Winston! Winston was my next door neighbor and he and his older brother Syral were my keys to the outside world. This may not be the best analogy but it was like those TV ads I saw as a child about the Iron Curtain. I lived in Eastern Germany in a sense and my two next door neighbors were the airlift from the West that flew in supplies for me to keep on living. I idolized those guys. They were older than I was. They were stars on the football and track teams at school. Their mothers would bar-b-que and have a backyard full of people over having big fun! They had cool things to say and their clothes fit. They were the big brothers that I never had and I loved them. They totally fit in!

I could always talk to Winston and one day I told him of my nervousness around girls. I told him that I felt so uncomfortable around others especially when they asked me questions about being different. I asked him, "What do you do to be cool when you want to talk to a girl"? He told me that when he knew that he was going to be talking to a girl especially a new girl for the first time he would drink one of his mother's beers. He told me that about 30 minutes before he called her on the phone he would just drink a beer. And then he said, "If you know a girl's phone number and you wanna call her I will give you a beer". I was scared out of my mind but I said yes.

I drank that first beer and I found the friend that I had

wanted to meet my whole life. I had a feeling like never before. I felt so good on the inside. My spirit just clicked and I was feeling alright for the first time ever! I felt golden! This was what I had been missing to feel whole! I had no idea that I had just begun a path to much misery. A path where I would hurt all the people that loved me.

9

So I'm thirteen years old and though I couldn't see it in my young mind I had already started acting like an addict. The little photo of the naked lady that I stole from the barbershop was not only my most prized possession but it also sent me on a quest for every provocative picture of a woman that I could find. The Montgomery Wards Catalog that my mother brought home one day quickly found itself behind my bed. I would take it out when no one else was at home and gleefully look at all the pictures of women in their underwear.

And then there was that beer thing. My father had started giving me a few dollars for working with him on the weekends and I began to scheme and plan on ways to get beer. But how could I not, it made me feel so good! Up until this point I was a lonely kid. I didn't fit in and I felt very uncomfortable in social settings. But now I had three of the best friends that I could have ever imagined. They were my own personal unholy grail and they made me feel warm, accepted, loved. No matter what else happened in my life I had my department store catalog behind my bed. I had the little photo of my naked lady and we were in love. And lastly I had alcohol. I felt like Jack Horner in that what a good boy I was becoming. Had I hit the jackpot or what! I had found a quiet place in my spirit. I was not lonely anymore. I began to think less and less about what others thought of me. I began to just like being alone with my photo, my catalog, and my magic potion. These new things added to my life would eventually cause me great pain. But for the moment in my adolescent life they gave me a sense of wellbeing.

By age fifteen I was gaining in confidence and I began to venture out further from my home and to take walks. I had a wide-eyed wonder about the world. My sheltered upbringing had kept so much of life from me and things taken for granted by most other were new awakenings for me.

In my home town of Orlando Florida there is a place named Lake Lorna Doone Park. This park is quite the historic landmark for Black people in Orlando in that for most of my young life we Blacks and people of color could drive past it but we could not go there. The park was so close that it was virtually in our Black neighborhood. But in reality it was a million miles away. But then Doctor King changed all that. By the time I first went there on my own it was open to everyone. There was a building in the park made out of beautiful large stones and we called that building the Rock House. There was a stage built next to the Rock House and this was the era of local bands. On Sundays the park would be packed with a couple thousand people. Black people all crowded around the elevated stage enjoying the battle of local bands.

One day I was in Lake Lorna Doone Park groovin' to one the local bands and I noticed a guy walking from the parking lot to the area of the stage. This guy would have a profound impact on my life. He was like no one else that I had ever seen. He had a body like I had seen only in comic books! He was extremely well groomed and his clothes fit him like they had been made just for him. Soon after this other people started to see him as he approached and it was obvious that many of them knew him. Everyone was so glad to see him and he knew just how to greet each one of them in the appropriate way. It was as if every guy wanted to be him and every woman wanted him to be her man. Needless to say I was in awe. I too wanted to be like him and to have what he had. He was respected and admired. He had confidence and sex appeal. I wanted that for myself! I was happy with the changes that I had made but after seeing him I wanted to go to another level! I no longer wanted to fit in. I wanted to be special. I wanted respect. I wanted the ladies to look upon me with desire. I was 16 years old and still very nerdy and gawky but I had just seen in the flesh what may be possible for me.

I later found out that this guy was a college football player that was home for the summer. I got to meet him one day and surprisingly he took a liking to me. I was shocked that someone so different from me would take the time to notice me. I would study him up close and see just who he was. I decided that I would make my body better. I would groom myself and get some clothes that fit. I would learn some cool greetings and so smooth things to say. I no longer wanted to just fit in. I wanted to be a man set apart from the crowd.

I had found a new addiction. That's what addicts do. I

had found something very important to me. See, there is no middle of the road for me. I either have no interest in a thing or it means everything to me. I am an extreme person. And I was becoming extremely interested in making myself special. I was going deeper and deeper into a world of my very own. I worked-out, I ate right, I groomed myself, I drank beer, and I got some new clothes. It was all about me!

I was still a virgin at this time but I still had the little photograph of my naked sweetheart. She went everywhere I did and was kept very nicely in my wallet. She loved me and I loved her. Her love for me was so great that one day she said to me, "Kenny, it's time for you to step out there and get yourself a real flesh and blood girl. You're a great guy! It's time for you to stop touching yourself and find yourself a girl". I listened to her and you know what, she was right!

10

I had worked hard all night long and I was bone tired. I was in that man-child stage of being 18. No longer a boy but not a man either. This was December of 1972 and all was right with my world. I was still living at home with my mother and my younger siblings, mom cooked every night, I drove her car out to the production plant for the graveyard shift job I had, and I was the big brother that my brother and sisters looked up too.

When I pulled in to the driveway that morning after working like a slave all night I just wanted to feel my body on my bed. I could eat later but right at that moment I just wanted to curl up under the covers and crash! Fate had other plans for me that morning.

Before I could turn off the key in the ignition Mother was at the car window. She said, "Go to the Loch Haven Art Center and pick up your brother! He is there in a concert they are having and he needs to be picked up". My younger brother was in a group called The Orlando Singing Boys. This was a group of 40 boys between the ages of 8 and 12. It was a racially integrated group and my brother was one of the four black boys that were a part of it. I had never been to the art center but when mom said that it was just up the street from Florida Hospital I knew that I would find it easily.

I get to the art center and it is decorated very nicely! This was about 10 days before Christmas and this was back when Christmas was still a big deal. They had pulled out all the stops and really did it up nice! I could hear the boys singing and a nice lady told me that they had about 30 minutes more to go before they would finish. I had never been inside of an art center before and I decided to walk around and look at all the fancy stuff they had in there.

I had been looking at the art for about 10 minutes when I noticed a man and an older woman watching my every move. When I would move to the next aisle they would move also. I could see them talking and they seemed to be talking about me. I had all kind of thoughts going around in my head. This was 1972 and though segregation was over, I was very much way on the other side of the tracks! In addition I am not dressed in what one would call art center attire. White uniform pants, black turtleneck pullover, and cement encrusted steel-toed boots. What could they be thinking and saying about me?

I turned a corner and we all came face to face. Their accent told me right away that they were from up north. They both said hello to me and began to talk about me as if I was not there. "He has a good face", the older lady said to the man. "Yes he does mother. Strong and dramatic", was the man's reply. "He has a good statue and he seems to be quiet fit", said the lady. They asked me if I was a lover of art. When I told them that this was my first time there they asked me "What brings you here today"? I explained about my brother being in the group singing in the concert behind us. They continued to discuss me as if I wasn't there. The lady told the man that she liked my clean-cut looks. She told him that she thought I was a good kid and that I spoke well. They explained that they were visiting from New York and would be here a few more days. Then the man asked me the most stunning of questions! He said to me, "We would like to test you, may we test you"? WHAT? They smiled when they read the expression of astonishment on my face. "We would like to take some pictures of you to see how you photograph. We will pay you for the sitting", He said.

I did sit for those pictures and the mother and her son liked them very much. As I was looking over the 100 or more photos that they had taken the lady's face lit up as if she had a bright idea! "Hey I bet Jim could use him ",she told her son! She walked to the phone and she and Jim talked. And just like that in less than a week I had gone from a guy driving home after stacking sacks of cement onto pallets to having a modeling assignment! And I was not even looking for anything like this to happen! I surely did not think something like this would happen to me! But it did.

So I go the modeling assignment and it is for a large tuxedo company. In this assignment an 18 year old kid is wearing really nice tuxedos and a beautiful grown woman dressed in different lovely evening gowns is standing by my side admiring how good that tuxedo makes me look. Is this real? Am I dreaming or what?

I never went to the Prom when I was in high school either as a junior or senior. But that next year after my modeling assignment I was the King of the Prom! When those brochures went out with me modeling those tuxedos it was like I had been living in the dark and someone had turned on the light! Suddenly people wanted to know about me! Who I was and where I had come from? Many of them had passed right by me many times before that. They did not remember those times ever happening. I remember one day I was at the Colonial Plaza and a group of young ladies approached me. They wanted to know about me, did I have a girl friend and all. I remember being so shy and uncomfortable.

Needless to say I soon got over my shyness. My spirit changed and I began to become a new creature. I had been raised until the age of 12 in a little dark cage. After that I was let out of that cage and a collar with its chain was placed around my neck. And now all of a sudden everything was changing so fast!

I had lived as the overlooked one, the forgotten one, the invisible one, the lonely one. And then one day the naked lady that I kept in my wallet came into my life. Then I met alcohol and we have been best friends ever since! Then a stranger without even knowing it told me that I did not want to fit in but rather to be a man standing alone. And now I get a few modeling assignments and take some pictures and girls want to hold my hand!

The shy little skinny boy had become an all grow'd-up something or other. If I could have seen myself from the outside I wouldn't have known who I was. I was going in a new direction and I just wanted to feel good. If it was gonna make me forget all those things of the past then that's what I wanted to be doing. I had lived a lifetime of pain and I was not going down that road anymore. I was gonna have some pleasure. That's what addicts do! I had everything I needed. I had my friend alcohol. Real live girls wanted to know my name. They wanted to hold my hand. I wanted to test out my new body. I was 'bout to be off the chain!

11

Funny thing about my life is that no matter what happens or where I am that skinny little boy of my past is right there beside me. He's my constant companion. No matter how grand I sometimes get he's always there to remind me to stay grounded. Well, most times he does. I mentioned that I was about to be off the chain and I did! You've all seen a dog when its master comes home. I was on uncharted territory and I had several new masters. I had my best friend alcohol. I had a new body. I had real live girls. I don't even remember where I was the first time somebody handed me a joint but I took it and like we addicts do I liked it. I was an addict and I didn't even know that I was. I didn't even know what an addict was. I just know that I liked what I liked.

I had 12 years of this self seeking lifestyle and it was a grand ole time! I lived alone and my life was simple. Workout, get weed, get babes, drink beer, and get laid! I loved my life! I just knew that it would go on like this forever! But, something happened that brought about a drastic change that I could have never imagined. I decided that I needed one woman in my life. I felt like if

I looked at another naked woman without any feelings between us I would just die! I was so over it! I wanted a special lady to love. And I wanted that lady to love me back. I wanted to get married and settle down.

I knew just the kind of woman that I wanted for my wife. She had to have all the qualities that mom had. She had to be a great cook like mom was. She would be able to sew like mom could. She would know just what to do when I wasn't feeling well just like mom did. And, she would be sexy as hell and want to make love to me all the time! Is this a great wife or what?

And I would be the perfect husband! You see I knew all about women and what they wanted and needed. I understood them perfectly. Back when I was that skinny little 7 years old boy I was a big brother in the truest sense of the word. At that time I had a sister that was 2 years of age and a brother and sister that were year old twins. I was not only a little boy then but also an assistant to my mother.

One of my duties was to keep an eye on the diaper pail that was kept in the bathroom. There were no pampers in the early 60's and diapers were made of cotton.

Mother had shown me how to wash out the soiled
diapers in the toilet and to add them to the other used
diapers kept in the diaper pail. When the level of the
diapers in the pail neared the top I would put them in a
laundry bag. I would put that bag on the handlebar of
my bicycle and ride up to the laundry mat. There I
would wash, dry, and fold all the diapers to be used
again. I would be the only child in the laundry mat doing
any work. Mostly the laundry mat was filled with grown
women doing the family Laundry. This was the early
60's and children knew their place. We stayed in our
child's place and didn't look grown folks in their
mouths. So, I would do my washing and not look into
their grown folks mouths. But, I did listen to everything
that these grown women talked about. They would tell
me all that I needed to know about women. They
wanted a man to take care of home. They liked a man
who knew how to dress. They liked a man who knew
how to kiss. They liked a man who even if he had a
woman on the side knew how to act. They liked a man
who let everybody know that they were number one.
They liked a man who stood up for them. They liked a
man who knew how to put it on them and would. They

taught me well. I knew just what to do. I was 7 years old and I understood women. I took this understanding into my adult life. I would learn that what those women had said was not the whole story. I was so naïve. I was about to go on a journey and I had no idea where I was going. Not only that but I hadn't even pack anything. I just knew that I wanted a good woman to be my wife. And like a good addict I let my wants and desires take charge of where they would lead me. I thought that if I did the things that I had heard the women in the laundry mat say to do that I would be the perfect husband! God and nature would send the perfect woman my way and I would ask her to marry me! Then, we would live happily ever after! I would be perfect. She would be perfect. We would take our vows and it would just all work out.

Well, I did meet a lovely lady and she was just perfect for me! I courted her for one year and all was well. We had a wonderful year of dating! We went for walks together and held hands. We went on trips together and we had quiet private times. She was the girl of my dreams. I remember one weekend she had to work and I didn't. So on her way to work she brought me a big basket of fried chicken, some beef kabobs and an ice cream pie with a chocolate graham cracker crust. She told me that she had made all of these things with love so that I would be OK until she came by later on to tuck me into bed for the night. Wow! She was so sweet and loving and thoughtful and kind! She had to go to work but she wanted me to be well taken care of. And to top it off she was going to come back later on and tuck a brother in for the night! She had my little mind fully blown out. I was seeing visions of sugarplums dancing in my head. I wanted to see her every morning and come home to her every night.

And so, in the month of May we had a wedding and were married! Not long after we were married things began to change. I thought marriage was like dating only legal and proper. I had no idea that marriage was two people making a life together. I didn't know how serious marriage was. I didn't know that I had to be a constantly involved in this thing. I honestly thought that if I went to work and brought my money home then I was a good husband. Besides that, I didn't beat my wife. I didn't cheat on her and I never acted the fool out in public. I was a good kisser. I knew how to dress up and look good. I knew how to put it on her and I did! I was doing all the things that the laundry mat ladies said were what a woman wanted. I was about to find out that there was so much more about a woman than what the laundry ladies had talked about.

During my childhood I learned many little lessons about how things in life are connected. But somehow when I decided to take a bride and get married I forgot all of them. I remember when I was about 6 years old my father would take me in the car with him all over the place. Mostly we would be working but sometimes he would go to visit his friends. My father had come to America from Jamaica in 1952 on an agricultural visa. When he got here he didn't know anyone. He was from a little village way up in the mountains and at age 26 it was his first time away from home. When he got here he lived in a little camp that was in the middle of a sugar cane field. He was brought here to the U.S. to cut the sugar cane and to harvest it from the fields around the camp in which he lived. The conditions there were very harsh. My daddy told me that it was like slavery. Six day each week the men worked in the cane fields from sun-up until sun-down. Every morning and every evening they were given a big plate of yellow grits with a glob of grape jelly. On Sunday there was only one meal at noon. My father worked this way for two years and made $22.00 for all of his hard work. He said that each time they were to be paid they were told that the worked they had produced only covered their living expenses. It wasn't what he had hoped but he was just glad to be in America. He sent all of that $22.00 back home to his mother and father.

After I was born my mother and father and I moved to Orlando, Florida. Dad never forgot what it was like for him when he came to America. How he was so far away from home and family. How hard he worked and was not paid for all his great effort. How he was brought to America but never saw anything but stalks of sugar cane for as far as the eye could see. How alone he was.

There was a labor camp about 12 miles from where we lived in Orlando in a little place called Harlem Heights. The men at this camp were all black men from different Caribbean Islands brought here to do farm harvesting labor. My father would go out to the camp and talk to the men. He would take me along with him. I remember that dad would take our family to church early on Sabbath mornings and then he would go out to the camp and get a carload of the men and bring them to church. After church they would all come to our house for dinner. Then at sundown father would take the men back to the camp and they were so very grateful for what he had done.

These were simple men who were all very poor. They were all very grateful for the things that my father did for them but they had nothing to offer him and nothing to give. But, they found a way to say thank you.

This was around 1960 and at that time in Florida the business of growing oranges was King! Most of Florida was rural at that time and there were orange trees as far as the eye could see! The men at the Harlem Heights labor camp worked at harvesting oranges and crating them. One Sabbath morning when dad went to pick up the men there was a surprise waiting for him. When he got there they told him, "Brother Richards, we can't go with you today because there will be no room for us. We seven men have been planning to do something for you and your family". Then each man went and got the big basket of citrus that he had prepared for my father. The leader of this little group told father," We don't have anything but we appreciate you. We found these old crates and we washed them up and dried them. All week long we have held back some of the fruit so that we can give you our best"! Man, all those good ole delicious navel oranges and sweet grapefruits! I love tangerines and I remember that there had to be 200 or more of them! I ate myself sick but I still loved it.

I guess what I'm trying to say is that everything is connected. I wanted a wife but I didn't know how to be a husband. I was a hard worker who brought his money home but I was not one to go on adventures with my wife. Actually I knew very little about how to treat a lady when we married. I was a loner who wanted a wife. It never crossed my mind that there was more to know than the lessons learned at 7 years old at the laundry mat.

So I got married and I did what I knew. I worked hard and brought my money home. I didn't run around and cheat on my wife with other women. I kept in great shape and always had my wardrobe looking good. I didn't beat my wife or act the fool out in public to embarrass her. I tried to be a good lover and used all the tricks and treats that I had learned from my bachelor years. That's what a good husband did right?

Later on my lovely wife began to speak of things that I had no knowledge of or interest in. She would tell me about something called life insurance. I had never even heard of it. She would tell me about long weekend getaways. I had never thought of such a thing. I was a blue collar guy. She was a white collar girl. I was 30 years old at the time and I wanted to make love every night. She would say, "Honey I got a big meeting with the Crime Commission tomorrow and I will be making a presentation. I need to get to bed early because I need to be sharp"! All I needed to be sharp tomorrow was some good loving that night and a fat joint to burn in the morning. That was a winning combination in my book.

I was like a fish out of water in a marriage. I was a simple man with simple thoughts and desires. I was tired of a different woman every night. I wanted one good woman. A woman like my mom was only sexy as hell and crazy about me! Just sex me real good and take care of me if and when I get sick and just let me work and get money. What I didn't know was that she wanted a relationship something that I knew nothing about. In hindsight it should have been easy. All I had to do was take her somewhere nice every now and then and she would have gladly shared her tangerine with me.

13

I was demon possessed when I got married. No not by Satan's little helpers or the kind we see in Hollywood movies. I was possessed by all the little things from my childhood past that were still major unresolved parts of my young adult mind. I had been a lonely little boy in my childhood. I was the skinny funny looking kid that was left out and left behind. I was the eldest child in my family and I had no extended family or friends in my peer group. My own imagination was my beloved best friend.

In my imagination I was tall and strong. Instead of a face where none of the features fit I would be handsome. I had clothes that fit me well and were very stylish. In these early imaginings there would be this special girl. But, not just a girl but a wife! She would love me and hold my hand the way mom would hold my hand when she and I would cross the street together. She would rub my forehead and sing little songs to me when I was sick just like mother did. This special girl that I would marry would always lift me up when I fell and put a healing band-aid on my scrapes. She would also be a beautiful Goddess.

I imagined lying in a green meadow and she would come out of the mist and walk slowly toward me. Her lovely hourglass figure accented by the gentle swaying motion of her perfect hips. She would make love to me and take my breath away. She would gently caress my forehead and tell me that she loved me and that everything was gonna be alright. "Sleep now", she tells me, as she walks slowly back into the mist.

Over many times and trials I changed from the way I was in my early imaginings. I did become tall and strong! The features of my face would somehow begin to blend together. And I bought stylish clothes for myself and became quite well dressed. From the outside I had become a new man. Yet I still longed for the Goddess of the Green Meadow. I dreamt of her often and was determined to make her mine.

14

Mother and I were sitting alongside of the carport in a little grassy area just this side of the hedges. We were chatting about this and that when I said to her, "Mama, I'm getting married"! She didn't respond but looked out ahead of herself as if she saw something far off in the distance. I told her that I was 30 years old then like she didn't know it. I told her that I was tired of sleeping with every woman that would let me and that I was ready to settle down. Still she said nothing.

Now I don't know about other guys but here is a little something about me that is a little odd. When women talk to me I hear the words that they speak but I never hear what it is they are really saying.

My mother got up out of her folding chair and moved it so that we were face to face. She took my hands in her own hands and looked deeply into my eyes. And then in a way that only a mother can do she said, "Kenneth, you are my child and I know you. Son, you are not going to be happy with a woman keeping house for you". I was stunned. I just sat there wondering and dumbfounded. On the one hand I felt that she was insulting my intelligence and maturity. On the other hand I was wondering what was it that she knew about me that I didn't know about myself. In hindsight I so wish that I had been wise enough at that time to ask her what she meant. Mother had said "a woman keeping house". What my ears heard her say was "a woman doing housekeeping". I thought to myself she can do housekeeping if she wants but that is not what I want a wife for. I can clean and cook for myself and I surely know how to do laundry! My niece would tell me many years later that her grandmother meant "everything but housekeeping".

I remember an early sign of the "keeping house" began while we were still just dating. I had taken my wife to be over to some friend's house for beer drinking and laughter. There were 7 couples all sitting around talking and just shootin' the breeze when my buddy John asked me if I was ready for another beer. To my stunned horror and utter shock my wife to be informed John that I had had enough beer for one evening and would not need another! A silence came over the whole affair. It was like one of those old E.F. Hutton commercials on TV. Looking back that was the first evidence that there was gonna be a problem. I wasn't on drugs yet but let's get one thing perfectly clear. I was already an alcoholic and she was putting a wedge between me and my beer! This woman and I had known each other for less than a year and I already had someone that I loved! I had a golden lady that never let me down. She was so cold and refreshing when I put her to my lips. She gave it up so good and went down so smooth and easy. And she always stayed in her place just chillin' in the 'fridge. I would pull her tab or twist her top and she would always give me that familiar "Hey big daddy" sound. I loved her and she loved me.

One of these two ladies was going to be my wife and the other was my side piece. But the line was blurred. I couldn't see clearly which was which. My human wife had her loving moments but she also had complaints about some of the things that I did. She also had wants and demands. She would question the things that I had planned or thought that she had a better way. I remember one Saturday afternoon she said to me, "I've been thinking about us going up to Home Depot and getting some plants to put out around the trees in the yard. What do you think of that"? I couldn't even answer her. I had been sitting on the sofa drinking a malt liquor and thinking of the NBA Eastern Conference Finals that I would watch that night. It was Jordan against Reggie Miller. I couldn't be thinking about plants and flowers with the game coming on. I had not signed up on the marriage team for all this. I just wanted the Goddess of the Green Meadow. Where did all this other stuff come from?

In the days to follow I began to change and not for the better. My spirit was breaking and I started to lose my way. I had been happy with my single life. As a single man I had a simple ordinary life. I went to work 5 days a week. I pumped iron 3 days each week. On the weekends I enjoyed doing my grocery shopping and I always cooked two big meals on Sunday to last me through the week ahead. I would do my laundry and clean my little apartment. Every day I would roll a joint or two for myself and just chill. This was the early 80's and I had a red landline phone. My buddy's would teasingly call it the "hot line" because almost without fail a dear sweet lady in distress would call and I would promptly invite her over. I was a doctor of sorts though I had no shingle outside my door. These damsels in distress would come over and I like a good psychiatrist would have them lie back on my sofa and share a little weed while I listened to whatever was on their minds. It seems that no matter what their concern was my diagnosis was the same. I would pour them a tall glass of white wine and ask them about their feelings. Then I would suggest that they allow me to kiss them softly and with tenderness from head to toe. I was concerned about their well-being like that.

But after several years of practicing medicine without a license and after rescuing many damsels from their distress I became bored with it all. There would be two events that were to change my thinking and my way of life.

I had over a period of time had built up a reputation for being this very fit and well groomed guy that was a freak. I had few hang-ups and almost anything a lady wanted to do or try I was game for. I tried every day to erase the loneliness and pain I had felt in my young years. I wanted to forget the young skinny funny looking kid that nobody wanted around. Surely beer, weed, exercise, and sex would take my pain away. I was an addict and I was addicted to them all.

15

There was a bug going around and I caught it and got sick. I had all the signs of being miserable. I had a fever and vomiting. I had chills and diarrhea. I couldn't even keep water down and it was coming out of both my ends. I was in distress and all alone in my little apartment. I was nothing like the guy who strutted around in well fitted jeans and tight shirts. Nothing like the brother looking to give out his phone number to ladies who might need some love. No, I was a stinky feverish mess sitting on the commode shaking from the chills all over my body. I needed somebody to help me but I was all alone. I know that this is not a pretty picture but I wished as I sat there that I had a good woman to come and look after me. The nerve of me to think that way when I had pushed so many nice young ladies away who wanted more than the sex we were having. These ladies wanted a relationship and I wanted to play doctor. Besides I already had a relationship with beer and marijuana. I already had a relationship with my inflated ego. I was in love with myself.

But, I was brought back down to Earth those 4 days that

I was sick. I had an out of body religious type experience kneeling on the floor of my bathroom. As I knelt there with my arms around the throne heaving my guts into it, my whole sinful womanizing life passed before me. And in a moment of clarity I could see the one woman that I had in my life who loved me. She was the only woman whose phone number I knew by heart. I called her and when she answered the phone I said, "Mama"! "Hey Son...you sound like something is wrong", she replied. Do I need to come over there"? These four days of sickness were the first of my two life changing events. Then the three day Christmas weekend of 1983 happened.

I love that part of each season from my birthday on November 7th through New Years Day. I love the coolness in the air that comes with November. I would celebrate my birthday on November 7th and then suddenly it would be Thanksgiving Day! The Christmas season would fill the air with songs and delicious treats everywhere and just one week after it would be the start of a new year! This was and still is my favorite time of the year!

When Christmas 1983 was just around the corner I was filled with the joy of the yuletide season. I was a 29 year old single man that had his own apartment and lived all alone. I had a little extra money saved and I wanted to celebrate and enjoy myself. So, about a week before the three day weekend began I told all of my friends to stop by my place while on their holiday coming and goings. My apartment complex was on the edge of a huge industrial park. I happened to work in the park for a large distribution warehouse that employed several hundred people. All around where I lived there were other apartment complexes and many of my friends and co-workers lived within walking distance of me. I had planned to have joy and to spread some holiday cheer!

I went to the deli and bought two huge meat and cheese platters. There was a lady on my job who baked very delicious cakes and I had paid her to make one for me. I ordered a smoked turkey. I had good breads and all the condiments and trimmings. I bought three cases of Moosehead beer. I purchased a quart of rum, a quart of gin, and a fifth of Seagram's Seven. I had an ounce of sinsemilla. This weed was so pretty it could have been a centerfold in High Times Magazine! This pot was so good that all you had to do was look at it and smell it through the ziplock plastic bag! Just that would set you off!

The Friday before that 1983 Christmas it was just another typical December morning if you lived in central Florida. I got my ten speed bicycle and rode the one mile to my job like I did every morning when I went to work. I had on shorts, T-shirt, and steel-toed boots. The air around me felt warm and cool at the same time as I rode to work. I was only going to work four hours that day as there was an option on my job to work all day on Friday or just to 11:00A.M. I was so happy.

When I left work that morning the temperature had changed and it had become very windy. I remember that my eyes began to water as I rode into the cold wind on my way home. Luckily I only had one mile to go. I put my bike away and knocked back a shot of gin. Then I rolled myself a fat finger sized joint of sinsemilla and got a beer. I couldn't wait for Sunday to get there. It was gonna be a great Christmas. Or so I thought.

They say that time brings about a change. Well, the

Thursday night before Christmas I had yuletide cheer on my mind. But, by the next evening it was getting really cold and Saturday morning it was cold as hell! Outside my bedroom window I could see the digital clock/thermometer that was in front of the Union Hall and it said 11 degrees! I wiped the sleep from my eyes because I couldn't have been reading the temp correctly! I had drunk a few beers and smoked a bit the night before but this was Florida! I knew good and time well it wasn't no 11 degrees! I put on my housecoat and went outside to see for myself.

The coldness of the air outside made me cuss. Even when I got back inside I cussed again! What in the hell was going on? This was sunny central Florida! I'm a Florida boy born in Fort Lauderdale and raised in Orlando. I remember when I was a small boy that the grown folks were all saying that it might go down near freezing one night but freezing is 32 degrees. The next day the temperature got up to 18 and it was windy.

Here was where my second mind changing event began. I had been through the four days of being sick and all alone in my little apartment 6 months earlier. Now, it was bitterly cold in sunny central Florida and I would spend the next four day alone in my little apartment. As I sat all alone the poem "Twas the night before Christmas" came to my mind because nobody was going anywhere or doing anything! The city was on lock! Nature had locked everything down and that's how it was!

I had had dreams of spreading yuletide cheer. I had visions of a sweet lady or two coming through and sharing their sugarplums with me. I had everything I needed to show anyone that came by so awesome peace and good will! But instead I was alone. Well, not all alone. I had food and liquor and some most excellent weed! And so, for 3 days and 4 nights I smoked out until I got the most incredible "munchies"! Then I ate like a pig! After that I would have a huge slice of cake and wash it all down with a shot of Seagram's Seven and an ice cold beer. Then I was ready for a nap! When I woke up I'd have the hair of the dog that had just bit me and do it all over again!

I was an alcoholic and an addict I just didn't know it yet. What I was learning over these days and nights alone with my drink and my smoke was that partying alone like that for Christmas is lonely stuff. As I sat there I saw this beer commercial where a sleigh was being pulled through the snow by a big dray horse. It was at nighttime in this commercial and a happy group of family and friends were together. Over the commercial there were people humming the song "Please come home for Christmas". The tenth time I saw it tears began to flow down my face.

I began to search my soul. When I looked inside I saw a very different man than the one I showed to the world. On the outside I did everything I could to look strong and confident. I lived like some kind of score was being kept and I wanted everyone to know that I was in the game. I took my vitamins and stayed fit. Surely those who I had wanted to impress would give me points for that! I worked hard and I was self sufficient. I had shown others that I didn't need them. I wonder how many points they would give me for that. I was so proud of the number of woman who came over and got into my bed. A guy who bedded down a bunch of ladies would get a lot of points wouldn't he? What an idiot I was!

I was a young man in my late 20's but I was also 9 years
of age. I had grown up and my body was big and strong
but all of my childhood demons were still inside me.
Those demons would talk to me. They would say,
"Remember who you used to be? If that's not who you
still are then prove it"! The demons reminded me that it
was they who were with me when I was alone and
lonely. They told me how they had nurtured me and
made me who I was.

I had reached a turning point in my life. I had come to a
fork in the road and I would have to choose a new
direction. On the one hand I was addicted to my
demons and they had been with me for a very long
time. But on the other hand I was lonely and I was still
alone. I had sown my wild oats and I had a ball doing it!
But now I was tired of all that. If I was going to be happy
I would have to change my ways.

Then I got a bright idea! If I had someone to love I
would not be lonely any longer! If there was one very
special girl who loved me I wouldn't be alone anymore!
We would meet and we would just know that it was
going to be wonderful between us! I would be her

prince and she would be my princess! She would be so loving to me just like mom was and she would be gorgeous and sexy as hell! And I would be her hardworking stud muffin! It was going to be great! I would go to work in the mornings and she would go wherever it was that she went. At the end of our day we would meet again in our little love nest. There we would have supper and afterwards we would do the dishes together. I would ask her how she wanted to spend the evening and she would say, "Let's smoke a fat joint and drink a few beers"! We would hold hands and laugh at the silliest things. Then she would take me into the bedroom and love me until she took my breath away! It was going to be wonderful!

16

I have come to learn that everything in life whether great or small is connected to at least one other thing. At my church there is a family event called "The Blessing". When a baby is born into a member family that is a part of our larger church family there is a day of anointing placed upon the child. On this day the grandparents, parents, aunts & uncles, siblings, nieces & nephews, cousins, and family friends all gather around the altar and present this new baby to the Lord. After this the pastor says kind and loving words over the baby and its family and then he prays. Then the family turns to face the congregation and the father holds the child high for everyone to see as the pastor proclaims the wonderful new life for the glory of the Lord!

My sister and her husband had recently been blessed with a baby girl and at six months of age the time of her "Blessing" had come. Since it was an important family event I pulled myself away from my little apartment even though there was an important football game to be played at noon. I was addicted to football. Actually I was addicted to anything that I really liked. I would make an exception this time because it was family.

When I went into the church the usher sat me right beside a lady that I had never seen before. Well, when something like that happens I feel that it's my duty to find out who she is! I liked that she was tastefully dressed. I noticed that she had nice knees. When we stood to sing a hymn she was just the right height for me. She was holding the church hymnal and like I had seen my father do I reached to hold the song book so that we could share it together. When I did my hand touched hers. At the same time we turned and looked into each other's eyes. So as the church sang all the verses of "Shall we gather at the river" her hand was under the hymnal and my hand was under hers. I had come to church that morning to attend "The Blessing" of my niece and now I stood there beside an unknown lady with her hand in my own. I was singing about this beautiful river but my mind was on her lovely knees. I wondered how lovely the rest of her must be. Father forgive me.

I was excited as I stood there beside this lady! Something about the moment felt so right! I was experiencing a chance meeting with a lady that I could not have imagined would happen. I wondered who she was and where she was from. I had a feeling different than anything I had experienced before. It was like when I was a little boy and just before bedtime my father would come home and have ice cream for everybody. And yet it also felt like the time he came home and caught me jumping like some crazed acrobat in his bed.

Well I did get to know this lady and after a year she and I became husband and wife. I was so excited by this! I am a dreamer and I was now going to be able to bring all of my dreams to life. My dream was working hard all day and making love all night. My dream was drinking beer and watching sports. I was a caveman and I had captured a female of my species. I had added her life to my own and without even knowing it I wanted to lock her away from all others just for me. She was my little 4" square B/W photo come to life. I would not have to keep her in my wallet like a little boy. I would keep her in my apartment where I could openly marvel at her femininity. OMG...I could have my Goddess and drink beer while watching sports on TV! I could smoke weed and pump iron while she admired the perfect specimen I had made of myself! I could make love to her and explore every shy boyish fantasy that I had ever had! WOW...I could enjoy all of my addictions all at once at the same time! This was going to be great! And then I woke up or rather I was shaken awake by my wife's dream which was very different than mine.

I had become a married man but I had no concept of what that meant. I didn't know that we were to blend our lives together and become a team in that manner. I didn't have any experience with being a team mate because I had never been on a team. I was always the odd man out. I had for necessity sake learned to go it alone doing my own thing my own way.

Early into the marriage it became evident that my wife and I were very different. I was a homebody and my wife was adventurous. My wife liked many things and I liked only a few things. I was a hedonist and my wife loved color and texture and design. I was addicted to everything that I liked. My wife had a wider more vivid view of things. My view of things was work, smoke weed, have sex, drink beer, watch sports, have sex, pump iron, sleep, have sex, eat, repeat! It was like I was a robot that had been programmed to think and act this way. I was more of a machine than I was a man.

Then the "keeping of house" that my mother had spoken of began and it really bothered me quite a bit! My wife would question my ideas and would want to know how I arrived at many of my conclusions. She had many ideas of her own that were foreign to me. She thought that having a dining room table was more important than having my weight set stored there. She felt that the walls in the living room should have pictures on them. I pointed out to her the poster of Earl Campbell breaking away against the Dolphins. She said that Earl had to go. She had an idea that I smoked weed too much. She began to not want to kiss me if I had been drinking beer. She started to not want sex every night like it had been in the beginning. If this was "keeping House" then mom was right and I didn't like it!

Over time I would see more and more that mom was right. I don't know what it was about me that she knew but her assessment of me was on point. I was not happy with a woman "keeping house" for me. I thought that when I fell into love and got married that we would be true to each other but that we would do our own thing and meet in the middle. I felt that all the things that made my wife the person she was when I met her should continue and I should continue to be me. I don't have the will or the desire to control another person especially the woman that I love. My thinking was if she loves me she will just love me and not because I am twisting her arm behind her back. I thought that marriage was like a lifelong date where we both earned our own money, took care of our own personal issues and affairs, loved our families, interacted with our own friends that helped to make our lives whole, and met as husband and wife in the middle of it all for super quality time.

Marriage was beginning to look more and more like a battlefield and I was losing. I came into marriage with my heart and mind free and pure and laid it on the altar. I thought that it was going to be all sweet smelling fragrance and flowers. I was going to be a good husband and a good man. I would work hard and bring my money home. I would make love only to my sweet wife and protect her with my very life. And in my imaginings my wife would read me a bedtime story and tuck me in tight every night just like mom used to do. Well not exactly like mom would do it. You know what I'm trying to say.

But battlefield marriage was going on and I wasn't armed for battle. I didn't even know there was going to be one! I entered the Octagon with my church clothes on! The battle began and I had my good shoes on. I needed some different kind of shoes to be doing this. I needed shoes for a whole new ballgame! My wife started to have more and more things that she wanted me to do. I would find myself at furniture stores where she would ask my opinion on what coffee table went best with what sofa and chair combo. I had no idea what she was talking about. There would be family outings that she wanted me to attend with her. I was a loner and a homebody. Family outings were hard for me. She didn't want me to work out any longer in the living room. She said that I would be sweating near the new furniture and that maybe my muskiness would affect the décor of the "front room". I reminded her that when she met me I worked out in my "front room" all the time. She told me that didn't matter because all my furniture was stuff that I had bought second hand at garage sales or friends have given to me. "None of it matched anyway", she said. I felt totally disrespected.

In retrospect it had to have been hard for my wife as well. She was adventurous and liked many things. She saw the beauty and texture of things. The things that surrounded her helped to give her life meaning. She was an artist and liked to paint and sketch. She was an excellent cook but she also liked fine dining. Physically she had great bone structure and exceptional muscle tone. She was a college educated woman. All of these things made her very attractive to me and I fell for her very easily. She was a wonderful woman but I was all wrong for her. Her undoing was that like all arachnids I had set a trap and she had the misfortune of getting entangled in my web.

Once when I was about five years of age mother called me to the kitchen where she showed me a huge spider web just outside the window. As soon as she showed it to me I saw a large green grasshopper that was caught and struggling to free its self. I asked mom who had trapped it. It was then that she showed me the big spider up high in the corner of the web. After the grasshopper struggled for about an hour it got tired and gave up its fight. Then the spider walked across the web with such ease and grace and began to eat the tasty green delight. I didn't understand it then but I too would one day cast my own web. I caught and devoured many tasty treats and it was all so much fun! But I would get tired of it all and one day a woman unaware would fall into my web and when I came close she would turn the tables on me and I would become caught in my own web. I would struggle to free myself but I was no match for her. It was not her strength that kept me captive but rather that I was in uncharted territory. I was in a place where I was unprepared to be. But how can the trapper prepare himself when he has no knowledge of being caught.

I was in a very unhappy place and try as I might I could not free myself. I could feel the life draining from my mind and body. I could feel my spirit grow dim from the weight of my unhappiness. My heart was breaking and I was dying from grief.

In my despair I remembered a story about desert

Bedouins and what extraordinary Falconer's they were. To the untrained eye the desert is just a vast sea of sand but to those who call the desert home they know that the desert is full of life. Through the centuries the Bedouin has perfected the art of Falconry. He knows that with a trained falcon he can always get a meal anywhere in the desert no matter how far away from home he may be. A loyal falcon will go out on his master's command and circling high above the golden sand. It knows just where to find small animals just below the surface. The falcon will hunt for its master and bring home what it catches with one condition. Four times it will venture out and give up its prey but if it doesn't get to eat the liver, the kidneys, and the heart of that fourth catch it will not go out again. Had I become my wife's falcon?

Whenever I find myself in a quandary it is always on my mind. I mulled it over and over in my mind and finally it came to me that it's just math! I have always been good at mathematical word problems and this is just what the problem was! You see when we met and fell in love there was a whole lot of loving and not much living. But as time had gone on there was now a whole lot of living and not much loving. In the beginning she had sweet little nick-names for me and almost everything I said or did deserved a little kiss. She had a cute little wink that she would give me that meant she was ready to put some bomb lovemaking on me. Just the fact that she was with me seemed to make her so happy. And I was so happy to do whatever she wanted of me.

But there was to be trouble in our blessed union and cracks began to appear. One of the things that contributed to our problem is that I am more robot than man. I have a fixed personality and live in a very rigid manner. I am also a hedonist and live for pleasure. I don't have many pleasures but the ones that I do enjoy I am addicted to them all. I lived to serve my body and to supply its needs. I ate right, exercised, drank plenty of fresh water, and got lots of sleep. Not because I wanted to be healthy but because I wanted to stand out from the crowd and look super. I was addicted to having my own place to live so that I would have sanctuary away from the hustle and bustle of the world. In that place only the sweet voice of my own mind would be heard. I cooked for myself, cleaned up behind myself, paid my bills on time, and was responsible. In my mind and inside the walls of my life I had my own little Eden. All I needed was to add a woman to this paradise and a Shangri-La would be born.

Needless to say I was living in a dream world. I had longed for a woman to come into my life and bring me love. But you see what had happened was she did come and after play acting along with me in my fantasy she suddenly pulled back the curtains and the bright light of the full day Sun was directly in my sleeping face. She told me that she understood my dream but that it was not her dream. She explained to me that in her dream there were things that needed to be obtained. Almost overnight the nice car that she had was not good enough any longer and she wanted a newer one. We lived in a nice part of town but the apartment that we lived in just wasn't enough. She wanted a house to live in because of some "nesting instinct" she kept telling me about. And to make matters worse she was like an old 45 record disk and I was 33 and a third. I was out of my element and I was sinking fast. My wife began to question me on everything. She would challenge my thinking and my plans. I never asked her anything. I told her to be who she was. She wanted me to be everything but the man she had met. I don't remember the order of which happened first but we stopped talking and touching. My spirit just sank down into a deep despair. My life was not happy anymore. My peaceful sanctuary was gone. I was alive but dead inside. I would tell her that I felt myself dying. I wanted so badly to get away from her but it was like some otherworldly force blocked my path and I was bound by it to her. I wanted to die.

17

One day at work my supervisor introduced me to a new employee and the two of us hit it off from day one. We were about the same age and we had a number of things in common. He was a hard worker and I liked and respected that. Because I had been on the job for a few years before he started, I showed him the ropes and introduced him around the facility. We developed a friendship and whenever we could we would talk about many things.

One payday the two of us were riding in my car on the way to cash our checks at lunchtime and I opened up to him about my marriage and how bad I had been feeling. He didn't say much and just mostly listened to what I had to say. That following Monday he told me that he wanted to turn me on to something that I just might like. He told me that he had brought me something and that after work we could go check it out. He told me that it wasn't anything bad and that it would make me feel better. Well I was feeling so bad and so low that I was ready for anything.

After work that day he drove his car and I followed him.

We pulled up behind a store that had been closed all my life. I had seen the building but had never even been on the side of the road that the store was on. I got into his car and he reached under his front seat and took out a little eyeglass case. He opened the case and took out something that looked like the glass part of a medicine dropper. It was longer than a medicine dropper and it had a ball of brass wire in it like the kind you use to clean pots and pans. He put a black rubber stopper on it like the ones from science class in high school. Then he took out what looked like a square piece of flat white candy. "Watch what I do", he told me. He then put a small chunk of the 'white candy" on the end of the medicine dropper that had the ball of brass wire. He took his cigarette lighter and melted the candy just a bit and put the other end of the dropper between his teeth. "Pull slow", he said, and when he had put the fire to the candy that is just what he did. He held the smoke in and then let it out all at once and the smoke filled the car with a sweet aroma that I had never smelled before. He sat there for about 3 minutes and just rolled the glass tube back and forth between the palms of his two hands. Finally he turned to me and asked me if I was ready. I nodded yes.

I took the glass tube from his hand and put it to my mouth. "Let me do your fire", he said. I began to pull on the glass and it was smooth. I had smoked marijuana and was accustom to the heat and the strength of its taste. But this was different and I pulled until my lungs were filled and held it in. I sat quietly and still just as I had seen him do. Way off in the distance I could hear a train coming. Not the modern day kind of train. What I heard was a train from the old westerns that I had watched on TV as a boy. I could see that old locomotive chugging along with smoke coming out of its stack. I realized that the train was no longer way off in the distance but that it was barreling down on me! It was so real that I would have opened my eyes to look if I could have opened them. And then suddenly that locomotive was my beating heart and I thought that it was going to come out of my chest!

And then it happened. A wave with a ripple effect started at the top of my head and went down to the soles of my feet. And I had what felt like a sexual climax all over my body that lasted a solid 5 minutes. I felt like an astronaut! What the hell had I just done!

Actually what I had done was to open Pandora's Box. I had done something new and different that made me feel wonderful! My innocent eyes were opened to a new sin. That part of my spirit that had been broken was soothed for the moment. I in a moment of folly had taken my first steps on a new road. But unlike Dorothy my road was not covered with yellow golden bricks. No, the new road that I had chosen to venture down was paved with brown turds. And there was no wizard at the end of my road but rather Satan himself.

18

I am different from most other people. A great many
people are born and are raised and do everything that
their parents tell them. Their parents share the wisdom
that they have acquired with them and they take it all in
and understand it completely. Most people are wise
enough to know that their parents know what they are
talking about. But, I am different from all of that. I
would sometimes think that I knew more than my
parents knew. I had no life experience but I just had this
innate ability to know just enough to get myself into a
world of trouble. And generally that's what I did.

I had been warned not to drink any alcohol. I had been
warned not to smoke anything. As a youngster a
movement called "Temperance" was a big part of my
life. At my church we sang songs about temperance and
the importance of a clean lifestyle. I remember one of
the lines from one of the songs we sang said, "Dare to
be a Daniel"! And I had tried to be like Daniel for a long
time. But, maybe his lion's den was different from mine.
Maybe in his lion's den he was not a shy skinny funny
looking kid that was always overlooked. Maybe his mom

had enough money to buy him at least one cool outfit that he looked good in. Maybe girls liked Daniel and he was suave and cool when he put his rap down. Perhaps Daniel wasn't a doofus dork at everything he did. Daniel probably wasn't an addict either but I sure was.

So when the day came and the guy introduced me to crack cocaine I had moved so far away from the teachings of my parents that I was already lost. I was like a golf ball setting up on the golf tee waiting to be clubbed. The years of beer drinking and weed smoking and sleeping with any woman who would let me had removed clean living from my mind. I hadn't been to church in years. I was so lost that I thought that Jesus cared about the big sporting events when they happened. I remember back in 1984 there was a TV game between Florida and Auburn and I said to myself that, "Jesus himself is watching this one"! Church service for me was my chair about three feet in front of the TV set, my Styrofoam cooler filled with beer on one side and on the other side a tray with about 6 or 7 joints rolled and ready! I was nowhere near being like Daniel. I remember that when I was alone in my little apartment that I didn't wear any clothes. I had to be naked when I walked in front of any of the numerous mirrors that I had. I had to make sure that I was who I had made myself into and not the skinny little nerdy guy I once was. Boy was I sick!

19

Mama always said that things were easy to get into and hard to get out of. I remember that I got into crack cocaine real slow and easy. My co-worker would bring a 40-block for me every Friday and I would do it on the weekend. I would wait until my wife was not at home and then take myself one real nice hit of it and put it away until the next time. It felt so good and I wanted to do more but I was afraid that I might go too far. I had a secret and it was going to stay that way. I made a plan for my crack smoking and I felt that I had everything under control.

In my plan I would never tell anyone what I had started doing. I would do it only when it was safe to do so which meant that my wife was away. I would always air the room out and spray some type of really good air freshener after I finished. I would always hide my little glass pipe and my crack in a good and safe place where my wife couldn't find it. And most important of all I would always act the same way I did before I stared to smoke my pipe candy.

My plan worked perfectly for about 6 months and then

something happened that changed everything! I went to work that Friday morning and when I pulled into the parking lot I didn't see my dude's car. As soon as I got into my work area the supervisor called a meeting. He informed us that our co-worker had been in a terrible auto accident and was in bad shape. He told us that we were going to have to not only do our jobs but also pick up the slack for our fallen comrade. I felt bad about what had happened to my work buddy and I said a little prayer for him. All morning long the welfare of my buddy was on my mind and I wished him well. Later on the supervisor passed out the paychecks just before lunchtime and it was then that I realized that I was not going to be getting my shit! OMG it was Friday and I needed my crack! Of all the times to have an accident! How could my dude get into a wreck just before Friday!

Without even knowing it I had planned my weekend around getting my crack cocaine. I knew when my wife would be out shopping. I had some really good air freshener. I had gotten a new glass pipe and already had a fresh piece of Brillo in it just waiting for me to put something on it. I had a routine to fulfill and now all of that would be messed up.

I got into my car after work and I was depressed. I was driving down Interstate 4 and even though it was December I began to sweat. My stomach didn't feel right. My brain told my mouth that it needed that taste that comes from that first hit.

I was almost to my exit when I did something that would put my whole life into great danger. I decided that I would go and find some crack cocaine on my own. I knew that my dude lived on The Drive and even though I didn't know anybody over there that little white girl told me that it would be OK. I got over there and I couldn't see why they called it Mercy because it was anything but that. It was wild as hell looking to me. There were people everywhere. On the sidewalks there were people. On the staircases of every apartment building there were people. In front of every little building there were people. In the parking lot of the neighborhood store there were cars painted in every color under the Sun with big tires and crazy rims. There must have been a hundred young men standing outside that store and they had the music playing loud. Women wearing red, blue, and multi colored wigs strutted their stuff in what looked to me like shorty pajamas and spiked high heels. I knew I was in the wrong place but my white girl was calling to me and I had to go get her. I wanted a piece of her on my pipe and I wanted to taste her so bad.

I couldn't remember where my dude said that he lived but then I saw a billboard outside of this apartment complex with three palm trees painted on it. My mind started turning over and I tried to remember if he had told me it was Three Palms Apartments. Anyways there was a long line of cars going in on one side and coming out on the other. That crack was calling to me so I turn in and inched along with the other cars. In my right mind I wouldn't even be in this part of town but now I was parking my car and getting out.

As I started walking towards I don't even know where, I could feel lots of eyes on me. They all had a strange look in their eyes like they were seeing a ghost that was out of his mind. I was nervous as hell and all the people looking at me seemed uneasy as well. I knew that I didn't belong there and so did they. Finally a big dude said, "Who you is"? I told him that I was Ken and that I was looking for my dude. "What you want him for", he asked. I let him know that we worked together and I got my crack cocaine from him. "You the police", he asked. Before I could answer he let me know that he wasn't trying to go back to prison. He told me to throw my money on the ground and to stand under that breezeway. Somebody up on the breezeway made a sound and when I looked up they dropped two small chunks of crack which I caught. I got my ass in my car quick as I could and got the hell out of there. To that point this was the craziest and most stupid thing I had ever done. It was going to get worse much worse.

20

Long before I ever undressed a lady I would be a valet of sorts. Whereas the undressing of a lovely damsel in distress can be such fun, the dressing of a lady in distress can be hard work. Mother was 35 when I was born and after me she had my sister Gwen who later passed away, my sister Joyce, and the twins Randy and Ramona. After the twins were born mother did not lose weight as she always had done before. This time she gained a lot of weight and went from her normal weight of 155lbs. up to 255! This is where her distress and my valet apprenticeship began.

Every Sabbath morning as the family was preparing to go to church I would begin the process of helping my mom get dressed. I would begin by putting baby powder on her back. Then she would sit in a chair and I would put the nylons on her feet first and then roll them up her legs. Mom would say, "Be careful I don't want any runs in my stockings"! I did the best I could with my nerdy little 8 year old fingers and hands. Then the first of the three dreaded steps of dressing mom would occur. I don't even know what they are called but on the bottom of her girdle there were these little tabs that stretched down and I would hook the tops of the stockings to them to hold them up in place. I hated those little tabs! I would be fumbling with them and mom would be frustrated that it was taking me so long to get it right. After I got that done the second of the three dreaded steps would take place. The buckling of the shoes! Oh how I hated those little buckles on the side that you ran the little strap through! And those little holes in the strap that you couldn't even see they were so small! I know that Jesus was helping me get mom dressed. There was no way I was doing all this by myself. And lastly, the dreaded super brassiere. See, back in the day we used different words than we use today. Mother had a bosom and thus the need for a bustier brassiere. This was not the cute little bras that I would dream over in the Montgomery-Wards catalog. This was a grown woman bra with big cups and about 100 little baby hooks up the back. Now mind you that I could hardly tie my own shoes really well at this point but there I was fighting to get mom dressed.

We would get to church and mom would be showing me off to the other ladies who were her buddies. They would say, "Oh sister Richards, Kenneth is getting so big"! And mom would tell them how helpful I was to her and though she never said that she was proud of me I could hear it in her voice.

21

When I was 5 years of age father and I took a trip to Jamaica and it was then that I learned what being out of one's element was all about. We got on the BWIA propeller airplane that morning in Miami, Florida and two and a half hours later we were in Kingston, Jamaica.

Everything was so very different from what I was accustomed to at home. People drove on whatever side of the road they felt like driving on. Everybody was aggressive and spoke in a very harsh manner. They constantly told each other not to make them vexed. Women smoked pipes. If you wanted fast food you were given an ear of roasted corn with the burnt husk still on it. There was no running hot water. There were lizards of all colors and sizes everywhere freaking me out. Traffic came to a standstill so that a sow and her piglets could cross the intersection on the highway. We were downtown one day and a man pulled out his penis and urinated on the grass in broad daylight. No one paid him any mind. I was only 5 years old but I wondered to myself what kind of place was this? I was a foreigner in a foreign land.

Many years later I would take another trip to a foreign land. I would fly on this trip as well but not in an airplane. I would fly to this foreign land on a crack pipe and I would be propelled by the smoke that it would jet into my mouth.

One of the funny things about this new and different foreign land was that it was just on the other side of the city I called home. There were three distinct areas that I remember I would find myself in. And though they were but miles away from where I lived I never went into these areas. In my travels before crack cocaine I stayed on the main highway. All of my ventures were on the main roads. I was a man born and raised in the suburbs. Whenever I traveled about I went from like environment to like environment. I would get into my car and pull out onto the main road and drive straight to my job. I would get back into my car and drive that same main road back to my home. My church was on the main road. The places that I shopped were on the main road. All of my friends lived on the main road. In my hometown of Orlando, Florida my travels took me on Interstate 4, Highway 436, Highway 50, Orange Blossom Trail, Semoran Road, and The East/West

Expressway. I was a point A to point B kind of guy. Looking for or taking shortcuts never entered my mind.

But then crack cocaine came into my life and all of that changed. I started driving a new way. I began going to places that I feared being in. Just to the edges of these new places at first but it wouldn't stay that way. The rabbit hole was going to get way deeper than just on the edge. I was going to find myself in dark dank dirty little dope holes having sex with my white girl on whoever's pipe I could drop her on. She always tasted so good especially that first draw. That first rock and that first pull of her sweetness into my mouth and lungs felt so good. And what a lover she was! She would get all inside of me and make me come from the top of my head to the bottom of my feet. She would hold me and rock me back and forth in her gentle loving arms. Then just like that she would want to leave! Her whole personality would change. She would start talking to me. She would say, "Hey, I ain't no cheap thrill. You got any more money"? I told her that I had a few more bucks and her eyes would light up! "Well big boy you better go get some more! I wanna spend some time with you darling", she said with a smile.

I would go over to see her on paydays and I was only going to spend $50.00. It would be Saturday or sometimes even Sunday before she would let me go home. I would be driving with my car almost out of gas. I'd be hungry now and still in my work clothes from Friday and not one red cent in my pocket. I'd be cussing that white bitch, cussing my own ignorant ass, cussing life itself. Finally I would get home and my wife would meet me at the front door. That's when the real cussing would begin.

22

I was about to venture down into the pit. I had been raised about as far away from the pit as a guy could have been raised but that's where I was headed. I had been raised by both my parents and we all lived together in the same house. The first 17 years of my life I went to church every week. Many of those weeks I also went to Wednesday night prayer meeting. I sang solos in church and my mother would play the piano for me. I was taught about Jesus and his love. I was taught right from wrong. I was taught how to work and to do things the correct way. I was taught by my parents to be respectful and to have good manners. I was taught by my mother to stand up straight and tall. I was taught that my word was my bond and to always follow through.

All of these things served me very well when I was on the straight path. I had been given a method for living by my parents and for many years I followed their lead. But just as righteousness has the Holy Spirit, evil has its unholy spirits and that is exactly what cocaine is. Evil had started me nice and easy. In the same manner that

Jesus sent to us a comforter in the Holy Spirit, so evil also sends to us things to give us comfort. Early on that comfort was a little 4" square black and white photo of a naked woman. Later it would be alcohol in the form of beer. Then something as innocent as a store catalog with its pictures of women in their underwear would give solace to my young troubled mind. These things would cause me to venture out and see things that opened my mind to myself. Then I would discover myself and I wanted to be beautiful and to shine forth that beauty. That new beauty would lead me to the female form and them to me. All the while I thought that I simply was maturing. I was maturing but into what? I was being shaped and softened into a type of putty that was so pliant that when cocaine came my way I was shaped by it into a ghost of the person that I was meant to be.

I went from where I had been raised and I fell into a pit where everything was just the opposite of where I had come from. I had entered a foreign land and none of what I had been taught was how it was. In the new and foreign land doing wrong was the right thing to do. Manners were for punks and to have clout one did anything and everything that they were big and bad enough to do. The foreign land had its own language, its own values, and cocaine dollars was its currency. The more people in your family the more power you had. The more family members who had been to prison and returned the more clout you had. Prostitution was respectable work for women and if you didn't trick with the women in the area you were suspect. Anything to get you yours was alright. Going to jail or doing time was something they didn't want to do but it happened. That's just how it was. I meet that white girl and in a moment of vulnerability my dude put fire to her and I sucked her inside. Worse thing I ever did.

Cocaine took me by the hand and led me to this other world and I went with her. I went to this new world and I was scared shitless but I still went. I was so proper and straight that in the beginning I would hear the people say that I must be the insurance man who had come to collect on the policies and lost his way. My clothes were all wrong to be in the hood. The way I walked was all wrong to be there. I had manners and spoke with completed sentences. They would look at me with quizzical eyes. Their eyes would be saying "what manner of nigga is this"? Is this the mythical "Cracker-Ass-Nigga" that we have been told existed but have never seen? Before too much longer I wouldn't even know who I was.

I was on my way to a mis-adventure and it was going to be like dying and to be still alive. I wanted to stop but I couldn't. I had ventured into quicksand and the more I tried to get out of it the deeper I fell into the pit. Before cocaine I thought that truth and honor were things to admire. Before that first hit of crack I thought that a man's word was his bond. I had places in my mind and in my character that were lines that I would not cross. I had boundaries and limits to what I would do. Over time I would lose all sense of right and wrong. I would even lose myself and become a wondering nothing accepting anything that brought me one more dance with my sweet white baby.

23

Mother and father gave me food to eat and a warm bed to sleep in. They kept a roof over my head and clothes on my back. They took me to church every week and taught me about Jesus and his love. They sacrificed and sent me to private church schools where I went on field trips to interesting places and where I also played the baritone in the school band. They were very strict with me and disciplined me when they felt that I needed it. They laid down the law. But, they never talked to me. There was never any context to the things they did or said. The older I get the more I see that they loved me but I could have really used a little explanation as to why I was doing certain things that they demanded that I do. I would have loved to understand how their knowledge of the past brought forward into the present would affect my future. I wish that I could have known just how much of an effort they were putting into making my life better as I was young and going through it. I had great parents. They were two very capable and strong individuals who gave their lives for me to be all that I could. For most of my life I just couldn't see their love for me, their great caring for me and all of the sacrifice that they gave. In order for me to see all this I needed something to connect the dots so to speak. I needed somehow to be able to see just what my parents had given me. Smoking crack connected all of those dots.

One of the saddest things that I realized was that out in that crack world there were many people that but for crack cocaine they had no life. Crack cocaine was everything to them. For me crack was something that I did to ease the pain and grief I felt from being unhappy in my marriage. But I hated it with a passion. I didn't like what it did to me. I feared it and where I had to go to get it. I despised what I was becoming and the things it made me do.

But I had a sense that too many of the other people that were in crack world with me crack was like manna from heaven. They loved being in the area where it was readily available. They adored and watched over their pipes like a mother hen watches over her chick. When they had a large amount of it and a comfortable place to smoke it was like a religious retreat for them. Street level dealers were like messengers of light. Suppliers who had much weight or like they would say "In Power" were like Gods.

Being in a crack area was like seeing and feeling a living organism with a heartbeat of its own. It never rested! And from the first day of each month until about the 7th day of the month everything went into overdrive! The whole area was like a big pot of soup on the stove boiling hard from the high heat. Cars rolling through nonstop, dope boys slinging everywhere, prostitutes and tricks making hook-ups, players parked up and down the block in their tricked-out rides, police riding, lookouts posted up, errand boys hoping that a player needs something so they can get a rock.

Before I came to this foreign land I didn't have much understanding about my parents. I was just a guy born into life and not really having a clue as to where I had come from or how anything at all was connected to me. My parents loved me but they never said it. They had no problem telling me when they were unhappy with me or if I had let them down. They were strong to discipline me when they felt I needed it. They never told me that they loved me. I would have really appreciated that. My greatest desire is to love and be loved.

But after I left their teachings and the way of life they had prepared for me I would over time begin to see clearly just what they had given me. I would begin to appreciate the discipline that they had put upon me. I would hear in my inner soul them saying to me that they love me. That love would be a beacon of light to me coming out of the darkness. It allowed me to continue when I felt that all was lost. They taught me of a love that was bigger and stronger than even that which they felt for me.

My pain guided me to this distant place where everything was different than what I had learned. I was hurting so bad and I needed something to ease my pain. Looking back it was like at the appointed time a messenger of evil was sent to me to give me a temporary relief. This messenger brought to me crack cocaine and in a moment of great pain and misery I succumbed to it. Worse thing I ever did.

I had tasted something that you just don't back away from. I had let an evil spirit into my body and once inside it went straight to my mind. Over time it took control of me and took me to places and made me do things that I could not have imagined. Cocaine is a mean and nasty master. Cocaine made me lie and steal from my mother and father. Cocaine made me abandon my wife and children. It had me living on the street.

But my parents had vaccinated me with God and his love. They may not have raised me the way that I wish they had but they did teach me to pray. They gave me knowledge of the Holy word and even when all hope seemed lost I knew to call on Jesus. I knew that he lived and that he loved me. In my darkest hours I knew that one day he would come and save me. And when I could go on no longer he came. That is why I am here today. That is why I write this story. I write because I have felt the power of God's love. I have seen how it all comes together when the Divine hand is at work. I am a living witness.

24

There was a war going on and I was the prize that was being fought for. I like all other humans had been made by the divine hand. Even though I know this I wanted to do my own thang. I wanted to enjoy the pleasure of my body. I had my own thoughts and I wanted to explore and find out if I was who I thought I was. I wanted to move far away from that old skinny funny looking Kenny that I hated so much. I wanted to act and be grand, and only God is grand so I moved.

I was a vessel just like a pitcher or a glass that one might drink lemonade from. But unlike a glass I was alive! I had been given free will by my creator. I took my free will and even though I knew of God and his love I went my own way. I thought that I knew more than my parents knew. I was wiser than the things that they taught me. I didn't know it at the time, but in the moment that I chose my own will over the teachings of my mom and dad, I was taking my first steps to crack cocaine. God had his way, my parents taught me God's way, and I had my way. I did rock paper scissors in my mind about a hundred times and believe it or not my way won out every time. So, I packed up all my stuff in my mind and I stepped out in my own faith. There was a war going on and I had stepped over to the other side.

In a war zone there a casualties and where I went to was no different. I was in so much pain from being married and living a domestic lifestyle that I needed something to get that pain up from off me. I was married to a good woman but we didn't match. I was a father with two small children who I loved very much. I had a mortgage and other bills. I was in my early 30's and had grown tall and strong, but inside I was the same little boy daydreaming about that small black and white photo I stole from the barber shop. Legally I was a grown man. I went to work, I had my driver's license, and bill collectors called me Mr. Richards. But I was an addict. The bigger part of life that is learned from living a full life I didn't have. The maturity it takes to be a husband and father I knew nothing about. As a result I became very unhappy and was hurting all the time way down deep in my soul. I felt trapped. I needed relief.

So, when my co-worker turned me on to crack I thought that I had found the relief that I needed. In the beginning it was so nice to get a 40 Block and go smoke out. My dude would bring it to work and I could be a closet smoker. I was doing something deadly and illegal and still looking pretty doing it far off in the suburbs where I lived. Then I started going down into The Hood to get my own. It was like being in Beirut down there in the hood and everybody was soldiered up except me.

You see, I didn't know that the hood had its own style of dressing, its own language, its own values, and its own sense of right and wrong. I would go down there in the only clothes I had. I had no idea that wearing a blue hoodie that said FLORIDA on the front made me suspect of being "The Police". But, on the other hand a FSU or HURRICANE'S hoodie said that I was alright. I had no T-shirts with slogans like "Don't Ask Me 4 Shit" or "I Ain't the One". Besides, even if I did my walk wasn't right. As soon as I started talking the gig would be up. What I needed was one of those translator books you take when you go overseas. Then, instead of asking where I could get some crack cocaine I would have simply said "Hey, any happenings" or "Who doing sumpin"?

God's love was all around me because there was great

danger all around me. Without God's love I would have been eaten alive.

But like I was saying there was and is a war going on and each of us is the prize being fought for. Like in every war there are many tricks that the enemy uses to conquer us. There are undercover agents that appear to be on your side but they are anything but that. Evil can use almost anything to trip up the unsuspecting person. I remember once after about 7 years of my struggle with drugs that a co-worker asked me to give him a ride home from work. At the time I had been clean and sober for several months which was a real feat for me. My wife and I agreed that I should carry only $3.00 on myself at any time. I took my work buddy to his apartment and when I had stopped the car he gave me a $5.00 bill. I was driving along and all was well. Then a voice said to me, "Ken, you've been very good for a few months now and just one rock wouldn't hurt you. Besides, you probably are cured now! Go ahead and take that $8.00 that you have and go get yourself just one good hit and after that go on home". It's funny the difference between $3.00 and $8.00 to a crack addict. I had been good for months and people were starting to be hopeful about me again. Surely they must see that I am all better and all cured up! I would go and get that one good hit of crack! What harm could it do?

So, I changed the direction that I was going in and got onto a new street. If I had stayed straight I would have been home in 25 minutes. But, I made a left and drove about 12 miles in the other direction. I ended up on Quill Street. It was my first time on Quill Street and I didn't know anybody over there. Nobody over there knew me either. It was December just a few days until Christmas and it was cold. I was nervous while I was looking for a place to park and then I found one. I got out of the car and started walking up to a group of guys rolling dice on the sidewalk. If I had known better I wouldn't have but I wore my blue hoodie with FLORIDA written across the front with bright orange letters. As I walked up everything got very quiet and no one looked at me. Then a guy standing in the middle of the street calls to me. He asked me what I wanted. When I told him that I wanted crack cocaine I could see in his eyes that he didn't feel good about what I had just said. "Where your money at", he asked. I told him I had $8.00 and he showed me a handful of rocks. As I was

looking at all the dime rocks in his hand someone
standing behind me reached around and sprayed me in
my eyes and face. In a flash my face was hot and I
couldn't see. A hand snatched the money from my hand
and I stood there in the middle of the street blind and
on fire. Suddenly it felt like being hit with a hammer
right between my eyes. Seconds later I was hit
alongside the head and this time it felt like lighting.
Even though my eyes were burning I knew that if I was
going to live I had to open them. When I did it was just
in time to see the next blow that was coming right to
the middle of my face. I threw up both hands like a
boxer and began to catch blow after blow on my arms
and hands. It hurt like hell but I didn't care. I had two
hands and two arms, but one face and one brain and I
wanted to live. All the while that the fierce attacker was
swinging that wooden walking cane at me, others were
getting on the ground behind me and I would fall down
backwards over them. Every time I fell the attacker
would rush in for the kill. But I knew I couldn't stay
down on the pavement. I fell 6 times but I only touched
the ground once. Each time I tripped backwards I was
getting up as I was falling. I wanted to live and that

meant getting up.

Then I saw an opening that lead straight down the sidewalk and I turned and ran like hell. As I was running for my life a man came out of nowhere and ran at me from the side. At that moment my football experience came back to me and I lowered my head and shoulders and ran as hard as I could. He put his shoulder into my thigh but I was running for my life. I knocked him aside and kept right on running.

When I got a few blocks away I went to some people's house that I knew and they let me in. There was blood all over my blue hoodie and a big cut in the back of my head. As his wife cleaned up my wounds Mr. Paul said to me, "Boy, you real lucky! You the only somebody that them dope boys done jumped on over on Quill Street and the paramedics didn't have to come and get 'em"!

God had held me in his hand that night and his angel gave me a path to free myself. I easily could have died that night but I survived it. I survived with a broken hand, a gash in the back of my head, a deep thigh bruise, and no feeling in my front teeth. I had tried for years to stop this evil crack cocaine and now in one night of a terrible beating I could let it go. That was enough for me. Finally I was in a place in my mind, my heart, and my spirit where I could stop this awful way of living and return to who I was really meant to be. This was it and I was done with crack cocaine. And so as I drove home that night I was in pain but I was happy. I had had enough of this and I was stopping forever.

In the 6 months that followed I went to work and came straight home to my family. I would nurse my wounds and thank my lucky stars that I had not been killed out in them streets. The back of my head had a tender place that made me sleep on my side. The side of my left hand had a lump in it the size of a lemon and I had a deep blue bruise on my thigh that was there for almost 6 months. After that I didn't speak exactly the same because I couldn't feel my front teeth. Other than that I was fine! I had seen my whole life flash before me out there trying to buy crack and I wasn't going back to those streets ever again. I finally had the therapy that I needed to stop doing crack. It's funny what getting hit upside the head will do for a man. I started acting like a good family man. I began having quality time with my wife and kids. One day I looked up and I was singing in the men's chorus at church. Yes I had really turned over a new leaf!

I really believed that I was cured and that I didn't even have to think about staying clean and getting sober. I felt that the beating had set me on a path to where going back was not even a question. So, I let my guard down and I lay back just basking in the glow of being safe and sound at home far from crack cocaine and those mean streets. I knew that if I stayed in my on lane far away from Crack Street and all the little dope holes along the way that I would be fine. And I was fine for 6 whole months.

Then one night I was minding my own business just driving along Interstate 4 when my car broke down. Boy I tell you the evil one will use anything to get you off track! I put on the emergency flashers and began to walk to the closest exit which was just on this side of the railroad tracks. I was less than a mile from Front Street. As I walked that way I wondered to myself how it was that I ended up here of all places. I had told myself that nothing could ever bring me back to Crack Street and now I was about half a block away from it.

This was the same area that I had been jumped in. After a beating like the one I had taken seems like I turn and run the other way. Like a crack fool I walked right up to it once again. What the hell was wrong with me?

25

I was sitting in my car early one morning and I heard a woman coming up the sidewalk toward me. I could tell it was a woman by the sound of her house slippers sliding along in that rhythmic song that they make. I didn't know her but I could tell that she was looking for me. You see in Dopeville I was a rare bird. I could be trusted, I had a car, and my drivers' licenses were legit. She walked right up to my car window and said,"Hey, take me to the store"! I told her to get in.

I crunk up and pulled off from the curb. She was not my first but she would be my last. I was a great driver. I was practicing all the time. I took dope boys to go get their product. I took people to go apply for food stamps. At night I drove whores and tricks around to negotiate in my back seat. And I took boosters to go boosting.

The woman that I was taking to do some shoplifting was about to change my whole dope smoking life. I had a routine when I took a thief to work. I knew just where to park and wait. I knew how and when to pull up when they came out the store. I knew the right speed to drive and the right route to take when the deed was done. Today was going to be quite different.

We pulled into the big box store parking lot and I was about to drop her off. She told me, "No no not right here go and park"! In my mind I was going to sit back and wait for a sign that she may be coming. Then I would approach and meet her at curbside and push the door open so that she could just slide in and off we go. But, as she opened the car door and saw me just sitting there she said, "What you doing? Get out the car nigga you going with me"! As we walk together to the store she explains that I would have to be her man to make it work. "Just follow me and be my man, you'll be alright", she said with a wink.

I had been taking boosters to boost for years but I had never been inside myself. So, 30 minutes after I meet this woman for the first time ever, I am pushing a shopping cart and feeling all kind of weird as she calls me baby. And what an actor this lady was! We went from aisle to aisle and we had a conversation like a real couple who were happily in love. She would ask for my opinion about different items. She asked me what a word meant on a can of soup. As I looked over her shoulder to see the small print better she pushed her bottom ever so slightly into my crouch. Her doing that made me uneasy. Her doing that felt good.

And then as if she was my tutor she began to tell me just how she did it when she got her boost on. She told me that she would shop just like anybody else would. "Walk slow and shop baby! Put all kinda things in the cart", she instructed. She told me to be on the lookout for some type of bag or luggage that the store sold. Then, when the time is right put what you really want into that bag and just walk out the store. And so that is exactly what we did!

As we are walking to the car she puts her hand behind my neck and pulled me close to her and kissed me full on my mouth with her juicy lips. I thought I was in the twilight zone and I was! One hour earlier I was sitting in my car drinking a malt liquor minding my own business. Now I am walking to my car with a small suitcase full of stolen goods! To top it all off a strange woman that I do not know had just kissed me full on the mouth with her full sinful lips!

I never saw her again after that day but those few hours we were together put me on a different path. Things were going to change now and not for the better. It was going to be even more dangerous for me now because not only was I in Dopeville smoking dope but I was gonna be stealing now too. There would be no more middle man for me any longer. No longer would I have to wait for someone to ask me for a ride to the store. I was the both the driver and the rider and what a combination I was!

This was war and the other side had landed a salvo right upside my head. Bad enough for me to be out there where I was doing what I was doing. But now I had a new vocation! In one easy 60 minute application I had been taught just enough to get me started on a new and more dangerous misadventure. I started stealing everyday sometimes 6 or 7 times each day. I was out of my mind! I would find a store, walk in and get a shopping cart, fill that cart with all kinda stuff that I didn't want, put a bag in my cart sold by the store, slip what I really wanted into that bag, and walk boldly out the front door! WTH? It was like I was looking at a fool in 3D throwing his life away. I watched him and wondered to myself how he could be so stupid! It was obvious that God had blessed him but he just acted the fool right in God's face! I could tell by the way he spoke and the words he used that somebody had taken the time to teach him a thing or two. He had good posture and walked like he didn't belong over here where he was. Then as I was looking down at him he suddenly looked up at me and I almost lost my mud! It was me! The damn fool that I was looking down at was me! But how? What the hell had happened to me?

I had to do something and quick! After the beating that I had been given by the dope boys on Quill Street and now this riding around stealing and smoking dope day and night! This had to end and soon! That was it I quit! So I did sort of quit but there was a war going on and the evil side wasn't done with me just yet. I had a ways to go before I would be allowed to quit. There would be many more seasons to pass over me before the rescuer would save me. Surely he would come for me soon I thought I can't take much more of this. I had been taught to pray and believe me I did. I prayed and I waited for my salvation. I always knew that one day he would come.

26

I was doing bad and getting worse day by day. It seemed like every day I would fall just a little bit deeper into this mess that I had gotten myself into. I started going to places that I knew I should not be going to. Dealers, thieves, and prostitutes began to know my name. I had put that white girl on that pipe and she felt so good! She told me that she was an angel and I believed her. She tasted good, smelled good, and felt divine.

But then she changed. I wanted to be with her so badly that I started following her to places where my very life was in great danger. She would take me to these places and say to everyone, "Hey, look at my new fool! Don't he look stupid as hell"? And I did look stupid. Everyone else was dressed all in black but I had on plaid overalls and a pointed dunce hat. She had turned me out and I did whatever she told me to do. She clowned me every chance she got and I just followed her hoping to smoke her one more time.

I could feel myself slipping away from who I was but I didn't know what to do to stop it. I was in such a quandary that I felt I was being pulled apart. I was married to a woman that I wanted to get away from but I couldn't leave her. She was a good woman but just not good for me. I had tried many times to leave her and every time something would block my path. It was as if some other worldly forces had bonded me to her and try as I might I could not unchain myself from her. I had asked her to come into my life and she came. But her being in my life caused me great pain! In that fantasy world which is my frontal lobe I wanted a woman to come in but not too close. Laugh with me, drink beer with me, kick it with me, get jiggy with me, and do some bomb lovemaking! I in exchange would get up every day and go to work and on Friday bring all of my money home to her. That's a good plan ain't it? I thought it was!

Being married to my then wife was not giving me the fun that I wanted and so I wanted to pack up my things and hit the road. But it was like I was in some kind of sinister game where no matter which way I turned or what I did I could not get away from the cause of my pain. And so when my coworker said to me, "Smoke two rocks and call me in the morning", I thanked him and went directly and filled that prescription.

With all that said it was not my ex-wife, not my coworker, not my parents, not the people from my childhood, or the fact that I wear eyeglasses that caused me to start smoking crack cocaine. Plain and simply put it was me. I am the one who made a decision to let an evil illegal spirit into my body. I am the one who gave it control of my mind. Willingly I had become its slave.

In this moment in my life that was filled with despair I still had the one constant that had always been in my life. I still had my mother's love. Every time it looked like I just might kick this thing she would be there believing in me with all her might. I had been born into the Seventh Day Adventist faith and as is our belief the Sabbath begins at sundown on Friday evenings. I as a grown man had gone my own way and I worshipped whatever my mind told me to worship. Every day was the same to me but to my mother! Sundown on Friday meant that it was time to be with the Lord.

One Friday my mother called me and asked me to take

her to run some errands. At this time I had been struggling with my crack cocaine addiction for about 10 years. That morning that she called I was in one of those reprieves where it looked like I just might make it! I had been clean but not sober for about 6 months. I had been working steady and going to AA and NA meetings. And when the family saw me I looked like I was being a good husband and father. This gave mother hope that I would make it this time and her trust in me returned.

Mother always liked to sew and of course we went to the fabric store that morning. After we left the fabric store we went to the arts and crafts store. She was 75 years of age at the time and doing artsy things with her hands was who she was. She loved children and she loved doing the arts and craft thing with them! We were just making a day of it and I remember that we stopped and had a nice leisurely lunch just the two of us.

We were having such a good time together that I started to feel that maybe this is the time that I will be able to put this evil thing out of my life and turn it all around. Sitting there in the restaurant I remembered that mother liked Mr. Goodbar candy bars and those long sticks of purple and green bubble gums. She didn't even have to ask me I just drove the car over to where I knew we could get them. We had a good laugh when I pulled up to the little place just off of Division Street. She told me she wondered where I was going. Mother said, "Well, since we're here we may as well go inside and get something"!

When we got back into the car we both realized that it was getting close to sundown. She told me ,"Son, I want to make one last stop before it gets to late because I want to get home before the Sabbath. She wanted to go to the supermarket and so that's where I took her. When we pulled up in front of the store mother put $60.00 in my hand and said, "Son, run across the street there and get yourself a shirt and tie and come go to church with mama in the morning"! We were on West Colonial Drive and just across the street was a strip mall shopping center with two men's clothing stores. I sat there with what I know was a blank expression on my face and mama said, "Run along now and hurry and come back"!

Mother got out of the car and went into the store and I pulled off headed to the men's store just on the other side of Colonial Drive. As I was driving I couldn't see it but there was a worm hole or some other type of vortex because the road changed and when I became conscience again I was in a crack house freaking out and sweating bullets! What the hell had happened? What had gone wrong? How did I get way over here from Colonial drive?

And then the shittiest feeling that I had ever had came over me. It was dark on a Friday night and I had left my 75 year old mother stranded in a shopping center parking lot miles away from her home. I had crapped all over my mother for a few rocks of crack cocaine! I wanted to die! She loved me so much and gave me her all. I am her first born and I took her money with the Sabbath fast approaching smoked it up and left her an old lady to fend for herself in the middle of the night. I cried like a baby and called out to God. Please hear me God because I can't take no more! I had taken a terrible beating from those dope boys. I thought that after that beating I would give up this nasty evil spirit that I had let into my body. I just knew that after that I would be done with crack cocaine. Then I learned how to steal and I became a bigger fool than the one cocaine had already made me to be. Riding around day and night stealing and selling what I had stolen round and round in a stupid sick cycle. And now I had fallen to a place that I once could not even imagine. I had kicked mama to the curb.

I made a decision that I was done with crack cocaine. I had hit rock bottom and that was that. I was ready to receive my salvation now and I called on God to save me. Surely he would see my plight and send is powerful mighty power down and save his helpless child.

27

I had kicked mama to the curb. I had done something so wrong that I had not imagined it to be possible. How does one fall so low as to do a damn thang like that? How does one get up in the morning knowing that they had robbed their own mother and left her stranded miles away from home?

Well in my case I had decided that I would not follow the teachings of my parents. Instead of worshipping God I would make for myself my own Gods. I would worship the female form. I would worship the viewing of sports on TV. I would worship the drinking of alcohol and the smoking of marijuana. I would worship having my own apartment for sanctuary sake. And I would worship myself. I would spend my time working on my body with physical fitness. I would groom myself religiously. I spent a lot of time in the mirror. I mean if one is to be their own God then they gotta look good right? If one is going to worship the female form then you must be able to bait them somehow. Don't you?

I had my life just the way I wanted it and then one day I decided to take a wife. I was not looking to share a life together with this wife that I wanted to take. My life was going very well and like another possession I wanted to add a wife to my life. I wanted to be married but not too married. This wife that I would add to my life could do her own thing. She could have her friends and they could meet and do whatever they did before we got married. She and I would meet in the middle after all the work and struggles were met. The middle would be that quality time where we enjoyed each other and explored our passions whatever they might be.

I had been alone for all of my life and I didn't know how to be connected to another person. I knew how to be the outsider. I knew how to be the overlooked one. I knew how to be the one left out of the loop. I knew how to be my one and only friend. I had learned how to survive alone and that is who I was. I wasn't self-centered, I had been centered. That's what happens when you are all alone for all of your life.

In my naivety I thought that I could add a wife to my life

and it would remain the same as it had been before. Ours would be an uncomplicated love where we each handled our business. After running the rat race of making money and paying the bills was done then it would be party time! The cold beers would start to flow and the weed would be lit up! All clothing would be abandoned and the sex games would begin! Maybe even a sex toy or two. After all this was marriage right?

But, it didn't work out that way and when it didn't I lost my mind. I lost the quiet sanctuary of being alone. I lost the peace of not being questioned about anything I did inside the walls that I called home. I had a woman keeping house for me and I didn't like it.

So, I decided to gather my few little things together and to make a run for it! I did gather my things but when I tried to bolt I discovered that there were no doors. I was one who would haul ass in a minute but not this time! I just ran around in a circle inside of a maze. The more I tried to escape the worse it got. I rounded a different corner of the maze and the dopeboys on Quill Street whupped my ass real good. I tried a new corridor and a thief with a big booty and full lips taught me what she knew about going in them peoples stores. I backtracked and made a left turn into a part of the maze that felt like it may lead to the exit. But when I went down further into it I saw mama and I was shocked! Mama was so glad to see me. I told her to get ready and that I would be right back for her. But I didn't go back for mama. I just left her down that dark dank corridor of the maze. Being in the maze was bad but it was about to get even worse.

I had fallen and I was still falling. I had once upon a time been an upright citizen living an upright life. But I had let an evil spirit into my mind and body and I was far from upright at this point. I had told myself a thousand times that I was all done with this crack cocaine thing and every time it had been a lie. I could feel myself falling deeper into this crack life fecal matter and I just could not catch myself. I had made a line in the sand over and over and each time I would wake up well on the other side of that line.

I had grown tentacles from my being and they were connected to all kinds of places and things. I was too stupid and far gone to be afraid. So I would go anywhere with anybody who had some dope. I had learned the terrain and likewise the people in the terrain had learned me. I had become a hustler. I had several hustles and I got them on every day. The evil one made sure that I had a car at all times. I know this because people would just give my dope addict ass their cars. My friend James gave me a car. My sister gave me a car. My father gave me three cars. The evil one was slowly making a whore out of me and I became the most taxi driving ass dope smoking nigga in town. I took dope boys to go get dope. I took people to the food stamp office. I took boosters to steal. I took kids to school who had missed the school bus. And I drove working girls around at night so that they could trick with their johns in my back seat.

One of the working girls that I met was different from the others. She was fearless and could make money when other girls could not. She had the face of an angel and the heart of a lion. She was a slim drink of water with a sweet round plump booty the kind that they only grow in the hood. I had a car and she felt that she could trust me. She was stacked and fully loaded. We teamed up and rode out together.

I would be driving in the hood and see her walking. I would slow down and stop the car beside her and she would get in. She would ask me, "What I got in the trunk". I kept a little cardboard box in the trunk of my car and I had her things in it. I had 3 wigs, a mini skirt, a pair of blue jean "daisy dukes", some baby wipes, 3 pairs of bikini underwear, and some peppermints. She would tell me where and off we would go.

I had fallen but I was a long way from where she was. Listen to me dope ain't no joke! She was at a place that I didn't even know existed. She had a hardness that was nothing like the outer beauty that she had. She would tell me to pull up behind a building and too keep lookout for her. Then she would get out of the car and strip down to her birthday suit. In the meantime I would have already gotten the little cardboard box out of the trunk. I knew the drill and I would hand her the container of baby wipes. She would take a few wipes and wipe herself down all over real good. I would have one of my eyes looking all around to protect us. My other eye would be all over her. She was a bad girl but at the same time a very clean girl and what she would do next would try my frontal cortex and my medulla oblongata. She would get about 20 baby wipes and reaching behind herself she would thoroughly clean between her cheeks. Then with 10 more wipes she would clean what she called her "coota-pop". Every time she did this the freak in me almost didn't want any dope. But I was a crack fiend and though watching her was delightfully pornographic I still wanted crack cocaine. It would not be long after this that we would be smoking. She would meet some money and I would hide close by to make sure she didn't get hurt. Watching over her to make sure she got paid.

But wait I was a good church raised boy and I had a wife and kids. What the hell had happened that had me out here in the middle of the night valeting a crack whore and acting like I was some kinda pimp or something! I was getting more stupid and far gone day by day. I wasn't a thug or even a tough guy but here I was watching a woman's back so that she could trick I peace and get us some dope. Standing hid off in the shadows watching her trick show and making sure she got our money. My mind was being warped out and though I could feel it I didn't know just how twisted I was becoming. My whole world was upside-down. Wrong was right and day was now night. Nothing mattered any longer. Just stay alive long enough to run another errand or to steal something. There was only one rule and that was to get more crack cocaine and smoke it.

28

I had been praying and asking God to help me. I would call out to Jesus and ask him to do for me what I could not do for myself. I had put one little piece of rock cocaine on a pipe and now I was in a different land a long way from home. The indigenous people of that land would ask me why I was there. They would tell me that I didn't belong there. I knew that I didn't belong there but I was hurting so bad and I needed relief from my agony. I felt like I was a pawn in a game that was so big that I couldn't see the players.

I had been hurting for 17 long years and I so wanted my pain to end. But it did not end and I just kept on going down further and further. I had been an upright citizen but now I was fallen. I had been honest but now I was a liar and a thief. I once had morals but I was becoming more immoral every day. I had been a hardworking member of society but now I could not keep a job. I was the eldest child in my family and they once looked up to me. Now I was not welcomed at their homes. My father disowned me and my mother was heartbroken and ashamed. I would hear the whispers in the streets. They would say, "You heard about Kenny Richards, that nigga done went out, he gone"!

And I would call out to my Jesus because I needed him so badly! I would say, "Lord, please come and save me! I'm hurting Lord please come save me! Lord I been beaten, I've been robbed, I been in these streets hustling Lord, I been going into people's stores and taking their stuff, I been a "Do Boy" Lord running errands for anybody with some crack cocaine, I don't eat no more Lord, I don't sleep no more Lord, I'm just a foolish fool riding day and night trying to get more crack cocaine. Please help me Lord"!

I would finish my prayer and off I would go riding like the crack fool that I was. I didn't know when my salvation would come but I believed in my heart that one day my Lord would hear my cry and come and save me. But until that great physician came I would have to suffer with that evil spirit that lived in me.

One day while I was out there chasing that rock I met someone that would take me to an even lower depth than I had imagined. In the same manner that people who lived in this foreign land felt that I didn't belong, those who came to the area looking to score crack could see something in me that made them trust me. Their eyes would say come help me get some crack. And being that I was a crack fool I would go right over to their car and get their money and go get them some crack. Of course I would take a sizable chunk of it for myself but the mere fact that I came back with some crack made them feel good. It made me feel good too because I was about to get on!

Because I was more trustworthy than the average crack fool I had built up a clientele of visitors to "Cracktown" looking to score. One of my regulars came to the gas station one day and wanted a $100.00 block. I went to where I could get more bang for the buck but the dealer told me that all he had was $500.00 pieces and he wasn't breaking them for nobody. When I went back and told "my visitor" what had gone down he gave me four more $100.00 bills and told me to go get it. In my mind I was like DAMN!

You know those big white chocolate macadamia cookies

that they sell at 7-11? Well that's what it looked like only it was bigger! And it was smooth and hard and pretty! Have you ever seen how rice cakes look when they are stacked up inside that clear plastic bag that they come in? I handed the money to my dude and he told me to get it from another cat around the corner in a little hallway. I turned the corner and sitting at a little foldout table was a dude with about 10 of these "cookies" stacked up! He gave me one and I put it in my drawers. He told me to be careful and I hauled ass!

I was scared as shit but at the same time I was an addict. I had never seen a piece of crack that big before and all I wanted to do was to get mine. I'm walking and doing drug addict math in my head. I'm doing division and subtraction. I say to myself that's easily ten $100.00 blocks or more if you cut it right. I get into the passenger seat and hand it to him. He looks at it and cranks up the car and pulls off. I wasn't expecting this but I am a drug addict and he now has the dope. We get on the east-west expressway heading east. I don't know where I am going all I know is I'm going with a really big piece of crack cocaine! We ride further east in Orlando than I had ever been before. We ride out there where it's just trees and clear sky not even really anybody else on the blacktop but the two us. He slows down and turns the car off onto a little dirt road way out in the middle of nowhere. We go about a mile up that dirt road until we reach a clearing that has on it the largest house that I had ever seen!

So, it's about 2:00 P.M. in the afternoon and we are drinking Jagermeister and smoking rocks like a couple of Navajo chiefs when all of a sudden he stands up and says, "Come on let's go take a shower". The 10% of me that was still human told me that what he had asked me to do was wrong. The other 90% of me that was crack fool got right up and got into the shower. I started off lathering up with shower gel but it wasn't long before he came over to wash my back. He washed my back, my legs, my feet, and all of my private parts. He toweled me off and told me to lie down. He massaged my whole body with body oil. Then we had sex. I had gone with this stranger on a Friday morning and it was Sunday night when he dropped me of at the gas station.

I felt the worse than I had ever felt in my whole life. I got out of that car and I just started walking. I walked for 3 straight days without stopping. I didn't eat, I didn't drink, and I just walked and thought about who and what I had become. My mind was in total disarray, my heart ached, and my spirit was almost gone. I wanted to just die if this was what my life was to be. After walking for those three days I found myself at lake Eola and I sat down to rest a bit. My whole life began to past before me. I had been a good boy from a Christian home with good parents. My parents taught me right from wrong. I knew all of the Bible memory verses every 13th Sabbath. I had been a hardworking young lad who paid all of his bills on time. I had taken a wife but I was not the marrying kind. My marriage was not good for me and I wanted to leave but I could not. Some other worldly force had bound me to her and I became a tortured soil. I had put a piece of that white girl on a pipe and smoked her deep into my lungs. I had been beaten, I had been robbed, I had become a thief, I was a liar and a cheat, and now I had had sex with a man for crack cocaine. Right then and there I made up my mind that I would never smoke crack cocaine again! That was it I had had enough. I couldn't live like this and I wasn't going to even try.

At that moment a wave of refreshing water washed over my entire spirit. I had finally reached my lowest point and now I would be able to rise to the top. No more beatings for me and no more stealing. No more riding day and night going from one hustle to another. And one last thing I knew was that I would never have sex with a man ever again just to smoke some damn crack cocaine! All of it was behind me now and I felt a relief and calm like never before.

Then I awoke from my crack addicted dream and I realized that along with all the other demons that were already inside of me that I had just added a new one. I began to go to places where men wanted to meet other men. I would put on my whore's outfit and go to these places looking for whoever had enough money. How ironic it was that the same body that I had built up to attract the ladies I now used to attract men. Every time that I went it tore a little piece of my heart out of me. Each time when all of the money was gone I would fall on my knees and beg God to save me! I would get up off of my knees and I would tell myself that I would never do it again. But I was just standing up there running my gator. Then in a day or two I would be right back at it being what sin could only define. Every day I became a more tortured soul.

Then one morning my baby sister called me on the phone. I was shocked because she almost never called me. I get on the phone and she says, "Kenny, I've been hearing bad things about you. I've been hearing things that I refused to believe. They say you've been hanging out at sinful places and I would just brush it off as just gossip. But last night I saw you with my own eyes. I was on my way to do my paper route at 3:00 A.M. and you had on white jeans and a black muscle shirt". Then she hung up.

I cannot put into words how I felt at that moment. I can't form into sensible meaning just how bad I felt. This was my baby sister. I had gone with my dad that morning when we went to the hospital to pick her and my mother up when she was born. I used to hold the bottle so that she could nurse. I held her hand when she first was learning to walk. I would walk her to day nursery on my way to school in the mornings. She and I had a special bond. And now she was calling to tell me that I had broken her heart. I fell to my knees crying and calling out to God! Please Father please! Help me Lord! Save your child!

Finally, something had happened that touched my core being. I had to stop doing these awful things that I was doing and I had to stop being a fool for crack cocaine. As much as I loved myself I loved my baby sister even more than that! And where did she find the love to call me even after I had hurt her so? I was a worthless piece of thrash and I didn't deserve that kind of love. I couldn't answer that question but I did know one thing. I would never do cocaine again. Ever!

I had stopped the smoking of crack for about six months when and evil voice said to me, "You know, you don't have to do things with men to smoke crack. You smoked for many years and never even thought about doing that. You've been good for a whole six months surely you could go and just get yourself a "Twenty". Just get yourself a $20.00 piece and smoke it and then come on home". I thought I was all done with being a fool but I fell for that load of crap! I went right back out there because it was just gonna be this one time. Besides, I had been really good for a whole six months!

I drove down there that night and got myself a twenty. And when it was gone I was driving around hanked out feeling like a damn fool. I was driving down the road and as I approached one of those old sinful places of the past the car turned into the parking lot all by itself. I don't even remember walking but I found myself in the bar. It wasn't long after I had money and was off to find that white girl. She would always excite me so much and leave me so fast. I put her on my pipe and she let me taste her. I tried to make her last but she was in control not me.

When she was all gone I went crazy banging my forehead on the steering wheel and the back of my head on the head rest. After about five minutes of this violent head bashing I couldn't take anymore. I gave the car to a stranger and walked to the other side of town. I went to a city park and sat on a bench. That was it I couldn't go any further. I couldn't take any more pain. It had been 18 years now and I was dog tired. I was 48 years of age and that's really old to be out here in these streets. I sat on that bench looking out at the grass before me and I said to myself, "God if you won't come to me I will come to you". As if by some strange magic as the words were forming in my mouth my vision changed and I saw lying on the grass before me a broken green beer bottle. It had its neck and part of its body and a long pointed shard on one side. I picked up the bottle and I looked at my left wrist. There was a vein standing there waiting to be pieced and I jabbed the pointed shard into my arm but somehow I missed my target. So being more careful this time I took better aim but again I missed. After about six tries I realized that the vein somehow was moving. But how could that be? I tried the other wrist and each time I stabbed the sharp point of green glass into my arm the vein would move. I sat on the bench bleeding from both wrist but not the way I wanted too. I wanted to die and it was just trickling out. Then I remembered the time I had been given an I.V. and my head turned instantly to look at that spot on my arm. Right in the bend of my right arm I saw the most glorious vein and right away I cut it! There was no trickle this time! You have all bent down to drink out of a public water fountain that is turned up way to high. Well that's just how it was when I cut my arm. A thick stream of blood shot out about three feet into the air. I felt my heart jump in my chest like it was trying to keep itself going and then I fell on the ground. They told me that a lady on the way to work found me. I guess it wasn't my time yet. Maybe I had a book to write.

29

I had tried to go be with God. I had been hurting for so long and been in so much pain that I wanted to die. But that's not how it turned out. My father was still alive at the time and I went to him and asked him to help me get up on my feet. He thought about it for a few days and he told me that the Holy Spirit had told him to help me too stand again. I had asked him to get my lights turned on for me and to pay my first month's rent. Then he did something that I truly didn't understand. He gave me a 1988 blue Toyota Corolla and $2,500! He told me again that the Holy Spirit had told him to do it. His doing so blew my mind but who was I to question the Holy Spirit.

Dad had been very good to me and I was so grateful! This had to be a sign that all of the dark past was behind me. I got a job not far from my little one room apartment and just lived a normal life. My sister had given me a TV and I had gotten cable. I just went to work each day, came home and cooked my meals on my two burner hot plate, and watched TV until I went to sleep. On the weekends I went and got my kids and brought them over for a few hours. I was happy and my life was becoming more whole day by day.

Once you have had a history of smoking crack cocaine you can and will have dreams of going to get it and of smoking it no matter how long you have been clean. I have been clean for over 14 years now and I had one just last week. Actually they are nightmares! When I awaken from one of these crack misadventure nightmares and realize that I am not in a crack house but rather in my bed I am relieved and filled with joy!

One day as I was driving there was road construction and I had to detour. The detour took me right through one of my old crack smoking territories. As I drove through and saw the people I recognized many of them and they looked like death warmed over. They looked liked extras in a horror movie. I was about 7 months clean at the time and had had this time to be away from this living hell that these others were living in.

I was sitting on my sofa watching TV when a small voice said to me, "Hey, you're not like those others. They are real crack cocaine addicts but you just smoke a rock now and again. And look at how good you look! How can you look so healthy and be one of them? Now, I'm a conman and I should have heard that this was a con but this voice was good! I just sat there and the voice just kept on talking. "You know what sets you apart from those other", the voice was saying, "You're way more intelligent than all of them! You're on another level! Now you messed up last time because you didn't know what you were doing but you've learned the game"! My grandiosity was showing and I wanted to hear more. The liar seeing that I was hooked told me how sorry he was that I had fallen as low as to sell my body for crack. He told me to let all of that be in the past and to just use my new knowledge to do it the right way this time. Besides he said, "You got $2,000 in the bank"!

I took my sick stupid ass back down to crackville and it seemed like they had been waiting for me! I ran into all the people with the best dope! I got unbelievable deals! I meet new people and this meant I was going to new areas and doing new things! I had gone back down there on a Saturday night and I must have partied for a month straight. Then just like that the party was over.

When my senses came back to me I had a feeling so bad that to this day I cannot put it into words. But I will tell you that not only does the evil one con you but he also sends you what you need next to keep going down.

With no money in my pocket I drove over to the house of a dope dealer. He must have seen me coming because he just came outside and got into my car. He turned to look at me and said, "Crank up, let's ride"! I drove him way out in the country and we went to an area that looked liked time had stood still. In a clearing that had been hollowed out of the woods there were four wooden buildings that looked like they were at least 100 years old. There were several old junked cars around the property and an old work truck from back when oranges were king here in Florida. Matter of fact it still had some of the old wooden crates on it from long ago. The women sat on the front steps of the buildings and the men played cards and gambled. Everyone there had their hair braided up and no one had on any shoes. An old lady came out of a little house and walked up to the car. The whole while that she was approaching her eyes were on me. My dope dealing passenger chuckled to himself and told her that I was alright. She leaned down close to the window and took out of her bra a package wrapped in brown paper. It reminded me of how we would wrap our school books in brown grocery bag paper when I was in junior high school. She told us to be careful and we assured her that we would. I crunk up and we pulled out.

We got back to his place and he told me to come back in two hours. I damn sure didn't want to leave and come back for my dope but what else could I do. That was a long two hours but somehow I managed to get back to his place right on time. He gave me two match boxes filled with shake. It was sho' 'nuff worth the wait! I don't know how much dope he had cut down to get that much shake but I was glad that he had.

I began to run errands for other drug cats. Sometimes I took them to pick up a package. Sometimes I went and picked up food that they had ordered. Other times I took their grandmothers to go get their food stamps. My car was my whore and I was pimping her all over town. I remember once I drove for 72 hours straight. I just drove and ran errands and drank malt liquor and smoked rocks.

And then I started to just get too tired to keep on running like I was but I couldn't stop. It seemed like everyone knew my name and wanted a ride to somewhere. I was slowly losing my mind again and I was older now and feeling the weight of it all. Then the hunger pangs hit me and I realized that I had not eaten in awhile. I was so low and destitute at that moment that I just walked into a Winn-Dixie grocery store and picked up a pack of sliced turkey, a pack of sliced cheese, and just walked to my car a drove off. I had nowhere to go so I drove to the city park over in the swamp and went to sleep.

As I slept I heard a weird sweet voice tell me to just rest awhile and to listen as they showed me the way. The voice told me that I was special! The voice knew my whole dirty dope smoking history and told me that I was far better than all of that. It told me that I should not be in places where I could be attacked and beaten. It told me that stealing was beneath me and was for ingrates. It told me that selling one's body was for those with no mind at all. It said that despite all that I had done I was still better than all of the others. And then the voice cleared its throat and spoke very slowly in a whisper. It said, "You know Ken, you could kill someone and no one would suspect that it was you".

When I woke up I had a headache and I was very troubled by my dream. I got out of my car and walked toward the lake. I sat down on bench and tried to clear my head. I was thinking to myself why would I have a dream like that? As I sat there wondering about the dream I saw under a park thrash can what looked like the handle of a pistol. Being a bigger fool than I had been before I went over and pulled it out and sure enough it was a gun.

Then like some kind of programmed robotic crack fiend I started to calculate backwards. I had a gun, I could kill someone, and no one would suspect me. I was always good at arithmetic word problems and it started to kick in. Who had enough crack and money and warranted dying so that I could have a load of dope? Who trusted me enough for me to get close and do the deed? These didn't feel like the thoughts of someone who was special but once you start doing crack you won't be special anymore. And my life had turned into deep fecal matter of the stinkiest kind.

I knew these twins that had taken a real liking to me. They had a shop that they worked out of and they drove in from some little town somewhere at 6:00 o'clock sharp every morning. They knew the way that my car sounded and when I got to their door they would just ask me if I was alone. I always went alone and they would just open the door and let me in. Like clockwork 30 minutes after I arrived one brother would always send me to the store for a pack of Newport's and bottled water. When I came back they would just open the door and let me in. I decided that they were the ones. I was going to do it that next morning before I lost my nerve. Was I the nutchurian candidate or what?

I drove to a place about four blocks away from the shop and waited for 6:00 A.M. to come. As I sat there in my car a small piece of me that was still human was crying inside for me not to do this terrible thing. The whole larger dope fiend me was so ready to have a bunch of dope and a bank roll of money! I was stupid sitting there out of my mind.

Lucky for me some things are out of our control. The evil voice of my dream had me in place and 6:00 o'clock did come but the brother's did not. For two years I had seen them arrive each day like clockwork but on the day that my sickness was at its greatest they choose not to come. And as the Sun rose that morning my senses returned to me and I cried out to God for his mercy and goodness is everlasting.

30

I knew that he would come someday but I just didn't
know when. Two more years went by and I must tell
you that every day I found lower places to go to. Every
new morning I was lower than I had been the day
before. My salvation would arrive some glad morning
and all would be right. I would be returned to being a
good clean honest upright gentleman. But, in the
meantime I was lower than I had been before. I still had
my car somehow but I was a mess. I didn't bathe
anymore or brush my teeth. I still had clothes to wear
but they were all were filthy. All of my clothes were in a
pile on the floor in the living room of an abandon
house. I would go in and exchange one filthy set of
clothes for a fresh set of filthy clothes lying on the floor.
I didn't eat or sleep and I was very skinny.

The one thing that did not change about me was that I
would still pray. I would beg God to send his son Jesus
to save me. I would pray and ask Jesus when are you

coming to save me. I had been suffering with the evil demon that is crack cocaine for 19 years at this point and now when I prayed my words were few. I had two prayers and they summed up all that I felt and desired. I would say "Help me Lord" or "Save Your Child". I have since read that Martin Luther once said, "The fewer the words, the better the prayer". He was truly a wise man because I was now praying in a new way. All of the flowery salutations that I once began my prayers with were gone. I didn't end them with Amen like mother had taught me to do so many years before. I just said, "Help me Lord, save your child".

And I was tormented day and night. It was just me, my blue 1988 Toyota Corolla, the Sun by day, the Moon by night, crack cocaine, malt liquor, and my most wonderful guardian angel that kept me alive. I so want to meet my guardian angel one day. He or she really did their job! I had walked all through the valley of the shadow of death and today I am better than I was before I ever entered it. How can that be but that God and Jesus sent their angel to guard my life?

I had no day or night now because all of time just ran

together. One particular time by moonlight I had taken two seasoned professionals out on a stealing expedition. I waited in the car for them to return. I must have taken them to a dozen places and each time they returned saying that something about the places just wasn't right. Each time I pulled up in the parking lot and dropped them off I so wanted to hit a rock! Each time they came back with nothing my crackheart would sink with disappointment. Finally, I said enough of this I will do it myself. It's 3:00 A.M. and we are the only people at this store. I go inside and I don't see anyone. No cashier, nobody shopping, and no stock person. I walk the store like I'm shopping all the while setting out all the things I want to drop down my pants. With all the items I wanted to steal all in their places I was just about to circle around to make my drops when out of nowhere a store manager comes out and follows me close like he and I are in a marching band. He is right on my ass! So, I stop and walk in the other direction. He stops and continues to follow me. I remember he had taps on his shoes like a drill sergeant. I walked right out the front door and he followed me out to my car. He wrote down my tag number and in a voice that sounded like Gomer Pyle he said, "See you later buddy"!

I'm riding back to town disappointed but at the same time so glad that I was not headed to jail. As I drive the two that were with me are laughing at me and making fun of me all the way back to Beirut. I hear them but my mind is thinking about the fact that my wife and kids were asleep in their beds just blocks away from where this all went down. I get back to the block and drop them off. The laughing stops and they want to know if I am coming back. I Lie and tell them yes. The store manager had told me that he would see me later. He lied to. I knew that I would never see any of them again. Something clicked inside of me in those wee hours in the morning and I just knew that my salvation was near.

When the sun came up that morning I was down by the lake on Mercy Drive. I had to get help and I went right up to the door and knocked. A man came out and I told him of my great pain. I begged him to help me. He told me, "Sorry dude, I have heard this story before and I am tired of being lied too". All of a sudden something hit the back of my head with tremendous force! It was the very pavement that I had been standing on. I had not even felt myself falling but there I was stretched out on the ground. The hospital dude ran inside and in what seemed like seconds I was surrounded by paramedics. They were working on me frantically trying to keep me alive. When they had stabilized me all of them moved away from me except one. I will never forget this man. He was tall, trim and muscular. He had bright blonde hair and a thick red beard. I remember that he knelt down by my side and said, "Hey, hey you down there"! I tried to see him but I couldn't focus. "Hey you no good ass dope smoking nigger! Oh you see me good now don't you nigger? I left a dying man to come and save your sorry ass this morning, how you think I feel about that? You think about it"! I tried to be mad at him but I couldn't because in that moment that's just what I was. Then all the paramedics returned and took me inside. I took a shower and the staff gave me a hospital gown and some little plastic shoes. They told me to rest awhile and showed me to a little room with a small mattress on the floor. They gave me a cheese sandwich and a small carton of milk the kind I got in elementary school. A cheese sandwich had never tasted as good as it did that day.

31

My parents were always trying to do more and to be better for me and my siblings. It was 1958 and my mom and dad had heard of a house in a better part of town so they checked it out. We had lived in that old part of the black community back from when it was white society and then just on the other side of the railroad tracks there was us. The house we lived in was an old wood frame house that sat up on cinder blocks. The place where we would move too was called Johnson Village. Old timers told me that Johnson Village came about because in those days our military was racially segregated and even though they had plenty of on base housing black airmen could not move their families there. We could fight and die for America but we couldn't live in the houses made for fighting men and their families. As a result Johnson Village was born.

My parents heard through the grape vine that a military man and his family that lived there were shipping out to

Germany. As quickly as they could they checked it out and fortune smiled on them. They got the house and an agreement was made.

One evening dad and I went over to the new house to do some clean up and make ready for our move in. Of course dad was doing most of the work but where he could he made small work for me. I remember that we were almost ready to leave and dad said to me, "Come Kennet, take this little box and put it on the back seat of the car"! Let me just say that back then there were not as many street lights or outside residential lights as it is today and so at night it was really dark. I took the box and walked to the back door of the car. All of a sudden I heard a ferocious battle going on behind me! I heard the growling of an animal with killing on its breath! I could hear that swoosh sound that comes when something is swung through the air with great speed and power! I could hear something hitting that ferocious animal over and over each time making it more ferocious than it was before! I stood there just looking into the darkness before me and seeing nothing. Out of nowhere a hand was under my armpit and lifted me throwing me into the open driver's side window! I landed on the front seat and listened as the animal was beaten back into the yard that was next to our own. Dad opened the car door and asked me if I was alright. I told him that I was and he told me, "Just wait here while I finish up, me soon come".

Our new neighbor was a lady named Miss Ruth and she was very nice. Miss Ruth also had the first Pit Bulldog that I have ever seen. This was the ferocious beast that my father had fought in that darkness. As it were this dog didn't like males and it didn't matter if they were 4 years old or 400. But no matter the beast when you are near to the father. I was a little boy in the darkness but my father's eyes could see into that darkness. I didn't even know that danger was near but my dad was watching over me. For me to survive a battle had to be fought. But this was not my battle to fight. This battle was far too big for my little 4 year old body and mind. But daddy was able and this battle was his.

I recall hearing my father tell my mother what had happened the night before. He was sitting at the dining table as he told his story. He looked to the corner of the kitchen and got up out of his chair. As he took it in his hand he told my mother, "This broom is a good one, it is tough and strong". He swung it hard through the air a few times and I could hear the same swooshing sound that I had heard the night before. Watching him swing that broom around like that made me proud of him in a way I still today cannot explain.

Funny thing about that broom! Just one week earlier the Fuller Brush Man had come to our front door and mother had let him come in. This guy always had the coolest stuff! All kinds of gadgets and do-dads. He had lotions, potions, and creams. I would always stand close enough to see what he had in the suitcase he carried with him and far away enough for mother not to run me out of the room. I remember that he had with him one of mother's favorite items and she always got some. Mother straightened her own hair and she loved this product called Old 97. It was a tall glass jar of hair grease with an old fashioned train locomotive on its label. I can smell it now melting on mother's hair from the heat of the hot comb. And he also had an assortment of brushes for every occasion. This particular time he had a broom with him and he told mother that this broom was like no other ever made!

He told her that the bristle of this broom were made by a scientist and would last forever. He said that the handle was made of metal and was unbreakable. Then he told her that it had a color that would match any kitchen design. I think the color was the most impressive thing to mom because she said, "Oh, I see"!

But just like that many mysterious things happen in this life. A salesman comes to our front door peddling his wares. He shows my mom all the things in his suitcase of goods and along with some hair grease she buys a new fangled style broom. A few days later father and I go over to the new house and he gives me a small box to put on the back seat of the car. I with the love and faith of a 4 year old take that box and do as dad has said. Dad is standing in the outside doorway of the kitchen that leads to the car. I am looking forward into the darkness as I approach the car. I don't see dad watching over me but I know dad and I know that he is watching. Miss Ruth's pit bulldog knows that father and I are there but does not know us. Father and I don't know about the dog or that we will all soon become acquainted. Mother has bought a super duper unbreakable broom that happens to have a lovely color.

Mother and I know about the broom but father does not. Suddenly, the dog charges me in the darkness. Dad puts the super broom to the test. It passes with flying colors. It all seems so simple and yet how do all these things come together at just the right time in just this particular right way. It is as if an unseen hand that is much larger than ours gives us what we need at just the right time.

When that day had come and I could take no more it was as if a force bigger and stronger than myself took me in its arms and held me. When all of my wiggling and squirming were done it felt like some higher power knew that I was ready and pulled me up out of the deep fecal matter that I had been wallowing in and rinsed me clean. When all of my trying to use my intellect to figure this thing out was done, it was like a big unseen daddy came to my rescue. When I was walking into the darkness and had reached my lowest point the daddy of us all appeared and beat back the beast from wince it had come. This Divine Hand is why I am here today writing my story to you.

After this I received help from every direction! There

were no more barriers and all doors were opened up to me! My family came back to me as if some signal had told them that it was time. The best treatment in the world was given me as if I was a man of money and means. It was as if a path had been set out before me and everyone along the way knew that I was coming! I was treated like my father was a king or somebody really special! And though I could not see him I knew that he was there. I could feel his loving hands beneath me gently holding me up. I could feel his spirit and I knew his name. He is the great I Am.

ABOUT THE AUTHOR

KENNETH A. RICHARDS is a semi-retired senior citizen that lives in Riverview, Florida. He is a native Floridian born in Fort Lauderdale, Florida in 1954. He is the father of two sons. He and his wife Stacey have been married since May of 2015. Kenneth is an honorably discharged veteran of the U.S. Air Force. He is a graduate of Jones High School in Orlando, Florida (1972). He is the son of Randall and Omar Richards; two hardworking Christian believers in Jesus Christ.

Made in United States
Orlando, FL
05 June 2023

33814891R00104